AMERICA AND
THE WORLD REVOLUTION

Note: The first of the three sets of lectures on related subjects that are published in this volume were given at the University of Pennsylvania during the second session of the year 1960-61; the second set were the Beatty Lectures in the same year at McGill University, Montreal. The third set were given in February 1962, on the Weatherhead Foundation, at the University of Puerto Rico. It was an honour to be asked to give these lectures, and it is a pleasure to recall the kindness with which I was received at the three universities.

1 May 1962   *Arnold Toynbee*

AMERICA AND
THE WORLD REVOLUTION

and other Lectures

ARNOLD J. TOYNBEE

1962

OXFORD UNIVERSITY PRESS

New York and London

Contents

THE PRESENT-DAY EXPERIMENT IN WESTERN CIVILIZATION

I

LIGHT FROM THE PAST: THE EXPERIMENT IN HELLENIZATION

THE title that stands on this page is a tell-tale one. Let me imagine an archaeologist in the far distant future, rummaging among the debris left by a third world war fought with atomic weapons. By an odd freak of chance, my imaginary future archaeologist finds my script. The date is not written on it. But, if the script is still legible, the archaeologist will have dated it correctly by the time he has finished reading the title. It is dated unmistakably by the two words 'Western' and 'experiment'. Neither word could have figured in the title if the script had been written in my grandfather's generation. This was the generation of Darwin, Huxley, Carlyle, Tennyson, and that pleiad of New England poets and philosophers whose graves are in Sleepy Hollow Cemetery, Concord, Massachusetts. If any one of those eminent nineteenth-century predecessors of ours had been asked to set out his views on the future, his title would have been different from mine, and it would have been shorter. It would have been just 'The March of Civilization'.

The nineteenth-century observer would, in fact, have made several assumptions that seem hazardous, or even positively mistaken, today. In our generation we are able to see through these assumptions. We are not, of course, any clearer-sighted or any wiser than our predecessors were; but, as historians, we have an advantage over them —the automatic advantage that is given by the mere passage of time. Between their time and ours, another act of the drama of history has been performed. So we know, for certain, what has happened in this act, whereas our predecessors had to guess what was going to happen in it, and, being human, they guessed partly wrong —as we, in our turn, are likely to guess partly wrong about the acts that still lie hidden in the future in our time. One of the nineteenth-century Western assumptions that has already been challenged by the course of events is that our Western Civilization is the only living civilization which is worthy of the name. So our nineteenth-century predecessors would have found the word 'Western' in my title superfluous. The one word 'Civilization' would have seemed to them to be enough. The adjective 'Western' would have been held to be implied in the substantive 'Civilization', so it would have been left out without any fear that this might make the title ambiguous. Our grandfathers would also have rejected my word 'experiment' as being needlessly and misleadingly tentative. They believed that they were witnessing, and taking part in, a movement that could not properly be called an experiment, considering that, in their eyes, it was already an unmistakable success. Nothing, they felt sure, could now hinder this movement from reaching its objective. 'The march of civilization'. meaning 'Western Civilization', of course, was in their opinion, irresistible. Its triumph was a foregone conclusion.

The nineteenth-century title would, then, have been short and simple. But, as I happen to have the chronological advantage of living and writing in the twentieth century, I have been warned by the course of events to put in the two cautious words 'experiment' and 'Western'. Each of these words is the equivalent of a question mark. But the questions asked by the words 'Western' and 'experiment' are addressed to the future. So we can get no direct answer to these questions till what is now still the future has become the past. The future, so long as it remains the future, is a sheaf of alternative possibilities, most of them still unknown. The transformation of the future into the past is the process that fulfils a single one of these multiple possibilities and leaves all the rest of them in limbo. Till we have reached the end of the fifth act, we cannot know for certain what the denouement of the play is going to be. In fact, the future course of human affairs is not a field in which we can have the exact knowledge that is the ideal of the physical scientist —and of the humanist, too, when he is dealing with past human affairs.

If you were to ask a professor about the future, his proper professional answer would be: 'Not my subject.' But, unfortunately for the professor, or, perhaps I should say, really fortunately for him, he cannot be a professor without also being a human being; and one of the characteristics of being human is that one makes plans. Planning is possible because it is concerned with the future. The future is still undetermined. So a human being who

makes plans for the future has a chance of influencing
the course of events—a chance of making things turn
out better, instead of worse, from his point of view. However academic-minded a human being may be, he cannot
afford not to make plans. We cannot afford this in our private lives, as each of us knows from his personal experience. And we certainly cannot afford it in public life,
now that we have launched ourselves into the Atomic
Age.

But how is it possible to make plans about a future
which is unknown *ex hypothesi*? In planning, we make
the assumption that the future will be like the past, at
least to some extent, and that our experience of the past
will therefore, at least to some extent, throw a light on
the future that will make the future partially foreseeable.
This assumption is made as a matter of course by people
who are still in what we might call the 'pre-civilizational'
stage of culture. They take it for granted that their world
and their ancestors' world are identical. Since the recent
dawn of civilization, those human societies that have
entered on the process of civilization have been changing faster and faster till, nowadays, each successive
generation of novices in the art of civilization is inclined
to believe that its own experience is unique and that
nothing at all like this has ever happened before. Logic-
ally, this impression about our own generation's uniqueness ought to make us give up planning, on the ground
that our predecessors' experience is irrelevant and that
we have no other data on which we could base any fore-
casts. Actually, people in our stage of civilization are far
more dependent on planning than the primitive societies

are. The primitives can afford to take no thought for the morrow, because they can count on tomorrow's being a repetition of yesterday. On the other hand the process of civilization does not spell itself out in recurring decimals. Accordingly, if we gave up planning, our civilization would immediately run on the rocks. So, in practice, we have to act as if we believed, as implicitly as our primitive ancestors believed, in the relevance of the past to the future—though at the same time it is obvious that the utilization of the past as a key to the future is a much more complicated and tricky operation in our circumstances than it was in theirs. Let us try, nevertheless, to apply a piece of past experience to our present subject.

Mankind's present-day experiment in Western Civilization may, in truth, be unique in some respects. For instance, this experiment is being conducted on a literally world-wide scale, and, as far as we know, this is the first time that that has happened. Still, there have been other experiments with a range that has been nearly world-wide—nearly enough, at any rate, to make them relevant to a literally world-wide experiment. Take the experiment in alphabetic writing. This was initiated, about 3500 or 3000 years ago, in one tiny country, the present-day Lebanese Republic. Yet already the use of the Alphabet has spread to the ends of the Earth. This book, which I wrote in the Old World and which has been published in the New World, is printed in the Alphabet. And, if I had travelled eastward, to Peking, I should have found a celebrated example of alphabetic writing there. There will be readers of this book who, like me, have had the good fortune to have visited Peking and to have seen the Temple of Heaven there. They will remember the trilingual inscriptions on the walls of that beautiful building. Two languages out of the three—namely the Manchu and the Mongol—are written in the Alphabet. Only one of the three, the Chinese, is written in a non-alphabetic script. It is true that, today, the Chinese ideograms are still the script of China, Korea, and Japan, and that these three countries contain, between them, about a quarter of the population of the present-day world. It is also true that the Chinese people has been increasing in numbers, and has been extending the area that it occupies, ever since the dawn of history. A Chinese domination and colonization of the entire surface of this planet is one of the possibilities that the future may hold in store for us. At the same time it is also possible, and even probable, that the Chinese will have adopted the Alphabet in place of their own ideograms before they have spread very far beyond their present-day bounds, and in that event the use of the Alphabet would become literally world-wide.

The Alphabet was invented by the Canaanites. They also invented monotheism and discovered the Atlantic. Their surviving representatives are the Jews, and there is no other human society that has greater achievements to its credit. But the experiment in civilization that throws the greatest light on our present-day Western one is not the Canaanite experiment, I believe. It is, I think, the parallel experiment that was made by the Canaanites' Greek contemporaries. The familiar name for this civilization is 'Ancient Greek'. But that name is a double misfit. The people who created this civilization were really modern, not ancient, on the time-scale of the age of the human race; and they did not all of them speak Greek. Before the end of the story, they also included large numbers of Latin-speakers, for instance. So I prefer the label 'Hellenic'. Anyway, whether I write 'Hellenic' or write 'Greek', the reader will know now what I mean. For an historian's purpose, this 'Ancient Greek' or 'Hellenic' Civilization has one great advantage over our present-day Western Civilization. It is no longer a going concern; so, in this case, we do know the whole story.

I will plunge my readers into this Hellenic story by asking each of them to imagine himself to be a Greek business man, living and working in the city of Alexandria-on-Nile in or about the year 225 B.C.

In 225 B.C., this Alexandria was the commercial and cultural capital of the Hellenic World. The Greek dynasty that was then ruling Egypt, the Ptolemaic dynasty, had founded at Alexandria a royal academy, the Museum. And this temple of the Muses had enticed away from Athens at least two of the nine sisters: the muse of natural science and the muse of critical scholarship. As a commercial centre, Alexandria in 225 B.C. had a vast field of enterprise.

Alexandria's immediate hinterland was Egypt, and Egypt in 225 B.C. was one of the two chief agricultural regions in the western half of the Old World. (The other was Babylonia, the present-day 'Iraq.) Alexandria's wider hinterland in 225 B.C. stretched south-eastward as far as India and north-westward as far as the British Isles. India had been brought into contact with the Hellenic

World by Alexander the Great's raid on India a hundred years back. The British Isles had been brought into contact with the Hellenic World by the enterprise of Massilia, the present Marseilles, a Greek colonial city-state on what is now the French Riviera. Massilia had been founded, about four hundred years back, by the Asian Greek city-state Phocaea. Alexandria lay at the mid point of this expanded, and still expanding, Hellenic World. It lay at the south-eastern corner of the Mediterranean Sea, which is a gulf of the Atlantic Ocean, and it had through-communications by water with the Red Sea, which is a gulf of the Indian Ocean.

From Alexandria you could travel in 225 B.C. up the westernmost branch of the Nile to the head of the Delta, and from there by ship-canal to the head of the Gulf of Suez. Larger ships, bound for South Arabia, East Africa, or the west coast of India, sailed from ports on Egypt's Red Sea coast. In whichever direction our imaginary Alexandrian business man might choose to travel, he would have been able, in 225 B.C., to do his business in the Greek language wherever he went. In the competitive opening-up of the western basin of the Mediterranean during the first half of the last millennium B.C., the Greeks had carried off the lion's share of the spoils. The Greeks' Canaanite and Etruscan rivals had won only comparatively modest holdings in the west. On the east, Alexander had overthrown the Persian Empire, and had opened up its vast territories for Greek invaders, Greek colonists, and Greek culture.

Three hundred years ago, reckoning back from 225 B.C., the Persian Empire had annexed Egypt and had threatened to engulf the Hellenic World as well. In 225 B.C. the Persian Empire's former domain was an open field for Greek enterprise, and the native population was lying passive. To Greek eyes in 225 B.C. this human material looked like so much wax waiting to be moulded by Greek hands into an Hellenic shape. The Hellenic way of life was the only way that now counted anywhere in the Old World to the west of the River Indus. Greeks and non-Greeks agreed in taking it for granted that Hellenism was going to prevail, whether their feeling, in anticipating this, was satisfaction or regret. It was assumed that, from the Indus to the British Isles, Hellenism would continue to be the dominant culture, and the Greeks continue to be the dominant people, except in so far as non-Greeks might qualify for becoming the Greeks' partners by adopting their language and their civilization. In the city of Alexandria itself the Jewish colony from the highland hinterland of Phoenicia seemed in 225 B.C. to be well on the way towards Hellenization. The ancient and famous Phoenician Canaanite city-states themselves—Tyre, Sidon, Byblos, Aradus— were more or less Hellenized already. Even the barbarian inhabitants of remote Britain were now striking coins that were crude attempts at copies of those minted by Alexander's father, Philip of Macedon.

All this would make our Alexandrian Greek business man in 225 B.C. feel confident about the Hellenic Civilization's future. But this civilization also had its seamy side; and this was its political side. In the third century B.C. the Hellenic World was not only split up politically into a number of local states that were each sovereign and independent; the great Hellenic powers, and the smaller Hellenic states too, were constantly going to war with each other, and this bad habit dated back in the Hellenic World to the beginning of its recorded history.

Almost ceaseless fratricidal warfare had been the ruin of these Greek city-states round the Aegean Sea that had been the original nucleus of the Hellenic World and the creators of the great civilization that had been inherited from them by the vastly extended Hellenic World of the third century B.C. For a moment in the third quarter of the fourth century B.C. it had looked as if King Philip of Macedon had given political unity to the Greek states east of the Straits of Otranto. But Philip's son Alexander had expended the united forces of the Hellenic World on shattering the Persian Empire, which, for two centuries past, had given at least some measure of peace and order to the oldest seats of civilization in the lands between the Nile and the Indus. The political configuration of the Hellenic World that had emerged from Alexander's meteoric career had been a replica of the previous configuration on a far larger scale and with a far more powerful drive behind it. Down to Philip's day the international anarchy of the Hellenic World had been kept within bounds by the Carthaginian Empire on one side and the Persian Empire on the other. Since Alexander's day this anarchy had spread over the huge area that the Persian Empire had previously protected from it, and the economic resources of this area had been added to those of Nuclear Greece and of Sicily to provide sinews for wars between Hellenic states. By 225 B.C. these fratricidal wars on the new grand scale had already cost the Hellenic World some ominous territorial losses. In the far north-east a nomad people from the Transcaspian steppe had prised out of Greek hands the Iranian province of Parthia (the present-day Khorasan). On the far west the Greek states in Southern Italy and Sicily had lost their independence to a non-Greek power, Rome.

A contemporary Alexandrian Greek business man would not have liked contemplating these unpleasant political facts. He could not help knowing them, because Alexandria did a lively trade with Syracuse, the leading Greek state in the West, which had now become a satellite of Rome. But the Alexandrian observer in 225 B.C. would have refused to allow his optimism to be deflated. He would have pointed out, and this with justification, that, as a result of having conquered some fractions of Hellenism's huge domain, both the Romans and the nomad squatters in Parthia had become 'Philhellenes', or, in other words, had become converts to the only civilization that deserved to be called one. As for the inveterate Greek habit of fighting fratricidal wars, an Alexandrian Greek in 225 B.C. would probably just have shrugged his shoulders. War, he would probably have said, was ingrained in human nature. Human beings had made wars since the beginning of time, and no doubt they would go on making them so long as the human race continued to inhabit the Earth. Moreover, he might have added, the present-day Hellenic great powers could go to war with each other with impunity. Early Greek wars might have been the ruin of the old Greek city-states; but, unlike these, the new Greek monarchies had all the resources of Egypt and South-West Asia to play with. These non-Greek resources were theirs to squander if they chose. For the native populations, which produced this wealth by the sweat of their brows, were an economic asset but were not a political factor. In the words of a native poet who had seen the establishment of the Persian Empire, 'as a sheep before her shearers', the natives were 'dumb'.

Well, this would, as I see it, have been an Alexandrian Greek business man's outlook in 225 B.C.; and, if my sketch of this outlook is correct as far as it goes, it displays some unmistakable points of likeness to, let us say, a London business man's outlook in the generation of our grandparents. The salient features of the picture repeat themselves one after another. In the nineteenth-century Western picture there is the same perpetual round of fratricidal wars, and these are taken in the same spirit. That is, they are taken for granted and are not taken tragically. There is the same exhilarating background of shattered Oriental empires—stretching away, in the nineteenth-century world, across the whole breadth of Asia from Turkey to China. There are the same droves of apparently sheep-like natives, submitting with the same docility to being fleeced without attempting to turn and bite their shearers. The Japanese may be reacting rather differently, but Japan is the freakish exception which proves the general rule that natives do not bite. There is even the same slight loss of territory on one of the nineteenth-century Western World's fringes (a loss that is being far more than compensated for by the partition of Africa). The heart of one Western country, Poland, has been torn out by a non-Western country, Russia. This is a shame, but, after all, Poland perhaps barely qualifies for being classed as a Western country, and, anyway, Russia has already become semi-Westernized as a result of having annexed Congress Poland and the Baltic Provinces and Finland. In short, our grandparents were as optimistic about the prospects of the civilization that was theirs and is now ours as my Alexandrian Greek business man will have been about the prospects of his civilization in 225 B.C.

But now let us go back to our Hellenic history-book and turn a page. I am reckoning a hundred years to the page, so this next page will bring us to 125 B.C. and to the Hellenic World as seen by my first Alexandrian Greek business man's grandson. In one direction the Hellenic World has continued to expand in the course of the intervening century. Within the last sixty years, Hellenic war-lords from Bactria, north-west of the Hindu Kush, have re-invaded India in Alexander's tracks and have gained a firmer footing there than Alexander himself had gained. The Alexandrian Greek business community have been alert in seizing upon this new opening for trade. They have been developing the sea-route from the Red Sea coast of Egypt to the Indus delta, and have begun to learn how to make a direct passage with the aid of the monsoon. But these minor entries on the credit side of the Hellenic Civilization's account with Destiny are far outweighed by two portentous new entries in the debit column.

One of these portentous events is the loss of political

independence. West of Bactria and the Indus valley, all Greek states have now gone the same way as those in Italy and Sicily had already gone a hundred years back. The Kingdom of Macedon has disappeared from the map, and this is a portent indeed; for Macedon was the Greek state that had made history, two hundred years back, by temporarily uniting Greece and permanently breaking-up the Persian Empire. Macedon is now a Roman province; Greek Egypt is a Roman protectorate; and all but a fragment of the once vast Seleucid Greek Empire in South-West Asia has been partitioned between Rome and Parthia. Rome has annexed Western Asia Minor; Parthia has annexed Babylonia, which is the equal of Egypt as a granary.

The second portentous event is, if possible, even more serious. It is the native revolt. The native peoples have turned and bitten after all, and they have done it with a vengeance. The Egyptian peasantry, the Palestinian Jewish highlanders, the gangs of Syrians who have been enslaved and been exported to Sicily to be worked to death there on the plantations—all these, and other oppressed and exploited populations too—for instance, some in Western Asia Minor—have taken up arms and have proved themselves formidable. The Jewish insurgents are religious fanatics who have been provoked by a 'Philhellene' Jewish faction's attempt to Hellenize the Jewish temple-state at Jerusalem in collusion with the paramount power, which was, but no longer is, the Seleucid Greek government at Antioch. The Egyptian peasantry has been made aware of its latent strength by the folly of the Ptolemaic Greek Government at Alexandria. In one of the chronic wars between the Ptolemaic and the Seleucid power in which the Ptolemaic power was being worsted, the government at Alexandria, in desperation, had recruited Egyptian peasants into its army and had equipped and trained them in the Macedonian Greek way. This had been tried as a forlorn hope, but it had proved a brilliant success to the surprise of all concerned—not least, of the Egyptian recruits themselves. The Egyptian phalanx had routed the Seleucid phalanx composed of seasoned soldiers of Macedonian Greek descent. Since then, the Egyptian peasantry had been out of hand. They had discovered, by a stimulating experience, that Greek troops were, after all, not automatically invincible. The military prestige of all Greek powers had been deflated by the Egyptian phalanx's triumph at the Battle of Raphia, before it had been annihilated by Rome's repeated victories over Macedon.

The parallel between the Alexandrian Greek business man's outlook in 125 B.C. and our own Western outlook in A.D. 1962 is so obvious that it seems unnecessary for me to underline it. So I will now turn two pages, which will bring us to the year A.D. 75. Hellenic history will still be serving as a mirror for Western history; but, from now onwards, as you will realize, it will be reflecting, not our past or our present, but one of those alternative possibilities that, today, are still lying hidden in the womb of our future.

In A.D. 75 the outlook for the Hellenic World, as viewed from Alexandria, might seem at first sight to be rather less depressing than it had looked two hundred years back. In A.D. 75 Alexandria is still the commercial and cultural capital of the Hellenic World, but she is no longer the political capital of a great power. She is now one of the cities of the Roman Empire, and, though she is recognized as being the second city of the Empire after Rome herself, this does not console her. Her feeling towards Rome is like Edinburgh's feeling towards London and Glasgow or Philadelphia's towards Washington and New York. All the same, business at Alexandria has perhaps never before been so good as it is today, and that is thanks to two changes for the better—a political change and a technological one.

On the political plane the Hellenic World's age-old international anarchy has at last been brought to an end. What Philip of Macedon achieved for a moment has been re-achieved by Augustus, and this time more durably, as well as on a larger scale. By A.D. 75 the entire Hellenic World, from the Indus valley to the European and Moroccan coast of the Atlantic, has been consolidated politically into the dominions of not more than three empires. The Roman Empire has united the whole perimeter of the Mediterranean sea. The Kushan Empire, bestriding the Hindu Kush, has united all the territories of the ephemeral Greek principalities between the Oxus River and the Jumna. The Parthian Empire holds Iran and 'Iraq. Not one of these three great powers is Greek. The Kushans, like the rulers of the Parthian Empire, are descendants of nomads from Central Asia. But all three powers alike are 'Philhellene'; each of them is keeping the peace more or less effectively within its own broad dominions; and, though Parthia is not on good terms with either of her neighbours, her wars with them are neither frequent nor devastating. As for the Roman and the Kushan empires, they were good friends with each other—as well they may be, since they have no common frontier to quarrel over, while they do have a common interest in the growing trade between them. The sea-passage between Egypt and the Indus delta has now become short and quick and cheap because the art of navigating by the monsoon has now been mastered.

Monsoon-navigation has been the great technological discovery of the age, and it is opening up new worlds in the South Seas for Alexandrian enterprise. Alexandrian Greek shipping is now reaching and rounding Ceylon and is making for the Straits of Malacca. In this direction Alexandria's horizon has been pushed far afield in the course of the last three hundred years. But the improvement in the economic and political situation has had effects on the religious plane. Now that politics have at last been put to sleep, the inhabitants of the Hellenic World are finding their spiritual treasure in religion instead—and not one of the religions that are profiting from this shift in the field of mankind's interest is a religion that is Hellenic in origin. The springs by which the new religious current is being fed are Egyptian, Jewish, Syrian, Anatolian, Iranian, and Indian. And this is a presage of things to come.

These coming things have arrived by the time we have turned the next two pages. This has brought us to A.D. 275. At this date the three empires are all still in being, though the Roman Empire is only just recovering from a stormy half-century during which it had very nearly foundered. The insurrections of the under-world which had been a menace to the Hellenic Civilization in 125 B.C. have recurred. Rome's tremendous military and political power had repressed the under-world for four hundred years, but had not killed its will to revolt, because even the Augustan peace had done no more than just to take the edge off the under-world's sufferings and grievances. The revolts of natives and slaves that had broken out and been repressed in the last two centuries B.C. have recurred in the third century of the Christian Era in the form of revolts of peasants and soldiers; and order has been restored only at the price of appeasement. The urban middle class, which had been the carrier and the beneficiary of the Hellenic Civilization for at least five hundred years past, has now been ruined irretrievably. The proletariat is now in the saddle, and the Orientals and the barbarians have broken through the Roman Empire's frontier defences. European barbarians have sacked Athens; Zenobia, the queen, originally by Rome's leave, of the oasis-state of Palmyra, has momentarily made herself mistress of one-third of the Roman Empire, as far west as Egypt and Anatolia inclusive. The invaders have now been chastised and the gaps torn in the frontier defences have been plugged. But the breaches, though now repaired, have demonstrated that the frontier is not impregnable.

These events on the military and political planes have been melodramatic, but the decisive plane of action has been the religious one. In each of the three once 'Philhellene' empires a religion of non-Hellenic origin is in the ascendant by A.D. 275: the Mahayana school of

Buddhism in the Kushan Empire, Zoroastrianism in the
Neo-Persian Empire that has superseded the Parthian
Empire in Iran, and Christianity in the Roman Empire.
In the Kushan Empire the relation between church and
state is not a problem. The Mahayana is an Indian religion or philosophy, and live-and-let-live is the Indian
practice in the religious sphere. In the Neo-Persian
Empire the reigning Sasanian dynasty has made Zoroastrianism the established religion of the state, and rival
religions—for instance, Manichaeism and Christianity—
have been persecuted. In the Roman Empire the Government has made several attempts, during the half-century
of anarchy, to stamp Christianity out. How could the
government expect the gods of Rome and Greece to
rescue the Empire from the jaws of destruction if the
government tolerated atheism? But the persecution of
Christianity in the Roman Empire has had just the opposite effect to what the Government had intended. The
Christian Church's martyrs have won for the Church
publicity, prestige, and converts. In the chaos of a dis-
solving civilization the Christian Church has stood out
as something solid and something worth-while. Its opponents' estimate of its prospects is revealed by their
action. All the other religions and philosophies have now
sunk their age-old differences and have formed a united
anti-Christian front. They cannot conceal from the
Christians or from themselves that this closing of their
ranks is a forlorn hope, and their pessimism will be
borne out by the course of events.

Turn another couple of pages, and the picture as it
presents itself in A.D. 475 will show that the omens of

A.D. 275 have been fulfilled. What was once the Hellenic World cannot now carry that label any longer. It has dissolved into three new worlds whose hall-marks are not secular but religious. The domain of the Kushan Empire, which had been the eastern extremity of the Hellenic World in 225 B.C., has now become a corridor along which the Mahayana, issuing out of India, has seeped into Central Asia and, from there, has peacefully penerated China and Korea. Zoroastrianism has become the national religion of Iran and, in achieving this, has set political limits to its own expansion. Christianity has become the exclusive religion of the rest of the Old World westwards from Babylonia inclusive as far as the eastern shores of the Atlantic. The Roman government has capitulated to Christianity without having been cured, by this experience, of its belief in the efficacy of persecution; and in truth, on this second trial in reverse, the policy of persecution has proved a success. During the last twenty years of the fourth century of the Christian Era, all practice of non-Christian religions in the Roman Empire has been stamped out by systematic governmental action: the pre-Christian religions of the Mediterranean basin are now represented only by a handful of single-minded devotees. These are idealists, but they are also cranks, so their faith will not succeed in moving mountains, though it is considerably larger than a grain of mustard seed.

Hellenism as a comprehensive way of life is now dead, and the isolated elements of it that are still alive are those which the Mahayana and Christianity have found it convenient to appropriate. The Mahayana, in its passage through the Kushan Empire, has found in Hellenic art a vehicle for expressing itself visually. This Gandharan Graeco-Buddhist art will eventually carry its Hellenic imprint as far eastwards as Japan. Christianity's reception of Hellenism has been less superficial. Like the Mahayana, Christianity has drawn upon Hellenic art, and this common inspiration has impressed on Graeco-Christian and Graeco-Buddhist art an unmistakable family likeness. But, unlike the Mahayana, Christianity has also drawn upon Hellenic philosophy. The Mahayana had no need to make use of this intellectual element in the Hellenic culture. Indian philosophy is self-sufficient, and Buddhism had started as a school of Indian philosophy before it had become a religion as well. Christianity, on the other hand, has found the adoption of Hellenic philosophy indispensable. Its missionaries' last and hardest task has been the conversion of the educated minority of the Hellenic Society. This minority's education was philosophical; and, if it was to be induced to swallow Christianity, the pill must be sugared with an Hellenic philosophical coating. Moreover, in this last chapter of the story, many of the Christian missionaries themselves were ex-Hellenes who had had an Hellenic philosophical training. By A.D. 475 the native Jewish and Galilaean tenets of the Christian faith have been transposed into an Hellenic philosophical notation. The victorious Christian Church has paid for its victory over Hellenism by saddling itself with the Creeds.

As for Zoroastrianism, it has set its face against Hellenism, and Judaism has turned its face away from it. The Hellenization of the Jewish diaspora in the Hellenic

World, which had seemed a foregone conclusion in 225 B.C., has, after all, miscarried. It has been blighted by a military and political conflict between the Palestinian Jewish highlanders and the Hellenic great powers: first the Seleucid Monarchy and then Rome, the Seleucid Monarchy's destroyer and supplanter. On the military and political plane, the Palestinian Jews have challenged overwhelming odds and have brought upon themselves a crushing and conclusive defeat. But the victorious Roman government has not been able to prevent the Palestinian Jews from retorting on the spiritual plane. They have retorted by repudiating the Hellenic culture, and they will succeed in constraining the diasporan Jews eventually to follow suit.

Our aperçus of the successive situations in the Hellenic World in A.D. 75 and in A.D. 275 and in A.D. 475 have given us a glimpse of one of the alternative possibilities that may be in store for our own Western World. This light thrown by history is, of course, only a spotlight flickering over an ocean of darkness, and the chances are that this tiny circle of illumination will not pick out and reveal to us the particular possibility that is going to become accomplished fact. History is certainly not bound to repeat itself, and it actually fails to repeat itself perhaps more often than not. At the same time, history is also not bound *not* to repeat itself; and, since it *may* repeat itself, our past experience is always worth bringing to bear when we are peering into the future.

I will end this chapter by trying to sum up in one sentence the plot of the drama of the Hellenic Civilization's encounter with the rest of the World. Hellenism won a temporary victory over the World in an offensive on the military, political, intellectual, and artistic planes; the World made a counter-offensive on the religious plane; the World was victorious in its turn, and this time the effects of the victory were longer-lasting. I hope to convince the reader that this Ancient Greek tragedy has a bearing on our Western Civilization's prospects.

II

THE ATTRACTION OF THE
WESTERN WAY OF LIFE

TODAY the whole World is bent on being modern; but
this agreeable word 'modern' is a euphemism. It is a
substitute for the less agreeable word 'Western'. One
may want to adopt an alien way of life, or, short of
wanting to, one may feel that this is the only alternative
to going under. But it goes against the grain to admit
that one's own ancestral way of life is not adequate to
the situation in which one now finds oneself. The word
'modern' saves face, so it has become a holy word, and
it has brought along with it two other holy words:
'science' and 'democracy'. Every nation and every individual in the present-day world feels bound to lay claim
to being 'modern', 'scientific', and 'democratic'. To disclaim any one of these sanctifying epithets, and, *a
fortiori*, to disclaim the whole trio, would be tantamount
to confessing that one was wilfully putting oneself outside the pale of civilization and was deliberately choosing
to sit in outer darkness. So Fascists and Communists
insist that they are democrats; British Israelites insist
that they are scientific students of the measurements of
the Pyramids; and old-fashioned people like me insist
that we are modern. The three words are certificates of

gentility; but for non-Westerners they are also something more serious than that. They are talismans for
acquiring those novel and overwhelming forms of power
that have enabled the West temporarily to dominate the
World.

For the great non-Western majority of the human
race, being modern, scientific, and democratic are, then,
so many ways of going Western without avowing it. But
why does any non-Westerner wish to go Western? What
is the attraction of the Western way of life? The answer
to this question is the subject of the present chapter. I
could give the gist of it in the four words of a proverb:
'Nothing succeeds like success.' Having said that much,
I could stop and save my readers' time. But I suppose I
had better try to develop my thesis.

The success of the Western minority of mankind has
been the major event in the last two or three centuries
of the World's history. But, besides being a recent event,
it has been an unexpected one. In A.D. 1661 this Western
Society was just one among half a dozen societies of its
kind that had arisen in the Old World. It is true that,
by that date, the West had won the command of the
Ocean, and had thus made itself the potential master of
the whole surface of the planet. The Western peoples
had already discovered and monopolized the New World.
But in the Old World, which was the Western Civilization's birth-place, the Western peoples in A.D. 1661 were
still perched precariously on the tip of the European
peninsula of the great Asian continent; and it was not
yet certain that they might not be pushed right off even
this patch of Old-World ground. When, in A.D. 1682,

Qara Mustafa Pasha led an Ottoman Turkish expeditionary force westward, his objective was not merely to make a second Turkish attempt at taking Vienna; he was intending to carry the western frontier of the Ottoman Empire up to the line of the Rhine; and, if Qara Mustafa had reached the Rhine, the rest of Western Europe would surely have succumbed to the Turks sooner or later. In the sixteen-sixties the Turks were doing some preliminary battering along the Danubian Hapsburg Monarchy's eastern frontier; and, even on the far side of the Rhine, the sense of the West's common danger was still lively in those years. It was lively enough to move Louis XIV in the sixteen-sixties to send a contingent of French troops to reinforce the Hapsburg Monarchy's eastern defences, though the Hapsburg Monarchy was France's arch-enemy in the West's own family quarrels. The situation did not change decisively till after A.D. 1683, when the second Ottoman siege of Vienna had failed and when its failure had opened the way for a Western counter-offensive. Then, at last, the West was relieved from the pressure that the Osmanlis had been exerting on the West's eastern land-frontier for the past three hundred years. It was only then that the Western peoples could concentrate their energies on converting their already achieved command of the Ocean into a domination of the World.

It was also only then that Western natural science consummated its marriage with technology and thereby generated for the West a material power that quickly put the rest of the World at the West's mercy. A conventional date for this marriage is A.D. 1660, which is the date of the foundation of the Royal Society in England. The marriage between science and technology was indeed an historic event. It was a new thing in the World's history. Ancient Greek technology would never have aspired to the honour, and Ancient Greek science would have recoiled from the proposal in disgust. Ancient Greek science's chosen realm had been theory. It had eschewed practice as being the sordid business of vulgar artisans. In a more recent age the Greeks' Muslim pupils had had an inkling that science and technology had been born to be each other's helpmates, but Muslim men of science had been half-hearted in acting on this intuition. The working partnership between modern Western technology and science was perhaps a legacy to them from mediaeval Western alchemy. In any case, whatever may have been this partnership's origin, the achievement of it endowed the Western minority of mankind with a material power that has since been making itself felt by one non-Western people after another; and the effects of this experience have been dynamic. The first reaction to it has been alarm; the second has been emulation in self-defence. Within less than forty years of the foundation of the Royal Society, Peter the Great was making his self-educational tour of the workshops of Holland and England.

Thanks to Peter's genius, Russia was prompt in getting off the mark. She deliberately began to run a technological race with the West more than half a century before the Industrial Revolution got up steam in Britain.

By 1914 Russia had fallen behind the West and was made to pay dearly for this by Germany in the First World War. Since then, Russia has redoubled her efforts and has been rewarded by outstripping the United States in at least one field of technological achievement—the field symbolized by the sputnik and the lunik. Japan, in her turn, reacted with the same clear-sightedness and strong-mindedness when the Western challenge reached her, as it did eventually two hundred years after Peter's day. Other non-Western countries—for example, Turkey and China—were slower in reading the Western signs of our modern times, and, when they did reluctantly read them, they were less prompt and less resolute in taking action.

The shock that was given to China by the West's nineteenth-century impact on her has had no parallel in history up to date. For not much less than three thousand years ending in A.D. 1840, China held the view of civilization that the West held for about three centuries ending in, let us say, A.D. 1958, the year in which the Soviet Union sent the Sputnik aloft. China held, and this not unreasonably, that the Chinese Civilization was the only one worthy of the name. China, in Chinese eyes, was 'the Middle Kingdom', set off against a foil of barbarian fringes. Since the barbarians did not really count, China was actually 'All that is under Heaven' for practical purposes. And then suddenly China found herself at the mercy of barbarians equipped with a new-fangled technology. If the barbarians who had laid China low in the Opium War had been the continental barbarians from the Central Asian steppes, China might not have felt the humiliation quite so keenly. For China to be conquered even by the nomads was, of course, unnatural and improper, but, all the same, this had happened more than once in the past, so it was a disaster that, like famines and floods, had its recognized place in China's experience. It had also been her experience that her continental barbarian conquerors could be domesticated and assimilated. But her nineteenth-century barbarian conquerors were the South-Sea barbarians, and her experience of these, during the previous three hundred years, had inclined her to write them off as being both despicable and irreclaimable. The humiliation suffered by China for a century and more ending in A.D. 1948 is something that is perhaps unimaginable for those of us who are not Chinese. After having been bullied by the authentic South-Sea barbarians, that is to say, the British and the French, China was bullied by these barbarians' barbarian imitators, first the Russians and finally the Japanese. I find myself appalled when I try to estimate the strength and the grimness of the Chinese reaction that has now been provoked by a series of aggressions against China that filled the best part of a century of Chinese history. I have a foreboding that our twentieth-century Western World may be required to pay reparations at compound interest for the sins against China that the nineteenth-century Western World committed.

China could not have been bullied by the nineteenth-century West if the Western peoples had not developed their modern technology and had not turned it to military account. China's humiliations at Western hands,

and Russia's comparative immunity from humiliations of the kind, bring out, between them, the
reason why the technological element in the Western Civilization exerts the attraction that it does unquestionably exert today all over the non-Western
World.

Turning new tools into new weapons has been one of
mankind's unfortunate habits ever since the first stones
were chipped by the last of our pre-human ancestors.
Beating plough-shares into swords has been a much
commoner practice than the reverse. Since the tools produced by the marriage between science and technology
in the West were unprecedentedly potent, the Western
weapons forged out of these tools were irresistible when
they were pitted against the antediluvian weapons which
were all that the rest of the world yet possessed. The first
form in which the Western question has presented itself
to non-Western peoples has therefore been the stark and
brutal question: 'Are we bound to be conquered by these
mightily-armed Westerners? Or can we save ourselves by
learning, in time, how to fight the West with the West's
own new-fangled weapons?'

The people to whom this question presented itself
earliest and most urgently were the professional soldiers
in the service of non-Western governments; and this
explains why, in a number of non-Western countries,
notably in Turkey, army officers have been the spearhead
of the Westernizing revolution which the military impact of the West has eventually set in motion. In
Western eyes the leadership of a revolution is an incongruous rôle for military officers to assume. In our

Western experience our own army officers have usually been conservative-minded on the whole, and this not only in their attitude towards political and social changes. Even in their own professional field they have frequently shown a distaste for those technical innovations that have been thrust upon them during the last two or three centuries by the ever accelerating advance of Western technology. The application of successive Western technical inventions to the art of war is what has given the West its modern ascendancy over the rest of the World. Yet Western armaments might never have been intensified, and the Western ascendancy, brought about by this intensification, might never have been established, if Western professional soldiers had been left free to follow their own conservative bent in their own professional field. What a pity that the soldiers have been pushed, against their inclinations, into falling in with the march of technological progress. They have been pushed into this by civilian pressure. If only we civilians had had the sense to let the soldiers alone we might have been spared the successive horrors of mechanized warfare, air warfare, and atomic warfare. We might still be having our wars waged for us with the comparatively innocuous weapons of the Pre-Industrial Age: petards and arquebuses or, better still, long-bows and mangonels!

Our Western professional soldiers would never have forced upon us our present annihilating weapons if we had left them to their own devices; for within the two hundred and sixty-six years ending in 1949, the year in which the Soviet Union acquired the atomic weapon,

there was no pressure on our Western soldiers from
anywhere outside the Western World. From the date
at which the West forged ahead of Turkey in the art of
casting cannon down to the year in which Russia
detonated her first atomic bomb, the West was not confronted by any non-Western power armed with weapons
that were a match for those that the West itself already
possessed. But, of course, during these same two and a
half centuries, all the non-Western countries of the
World *have* been confronted by a more potently armed
West, notwithstanding the brake that has been put upon
the intensification of Western armaments by the conservatism of Western professional soldiers. No doubt,
non-Western professional soldiers are conditioned to be
equally conservative by the automatic and inevitable
effects of a military training. But, for the non-Western
professional soldier in the Modern Age, it has been in-
escapably evident that he could not afford to indulge his
conservative inclinations. He has found himself in the
front line, within point-blank range of terrific Western
fire-power. To remain conservative in these circumstances
would have been, for the non-Western soldier, a patent
dereliction of professional duty, and it would have been
more than that. It would have spelled self-condemnation
to a speedy death. It is therefore not surprising—it was
indeed inevitable—that modern non-Western professional soldiers should have become precocious revolutionaries.

The attractiveness of Western weapons for non-
Westerners thus presents no puzzle. It is tragic, but it is
also rational. It is rational because there is no denying

that the strategy of fighting the West with its own weapons has been the only means by which the non-Western majority of mankind has been able to save itself from falling under Western domination, or has been able to extricate itself from Western domination after having fallen under it. Moreover, the acquisition of weapons more potent than one's own, and the mastery of the use of them, are achievements that appeal to irrational human impulses as well. It is human to hate finding oneself in the power of a neighbour for whom one is no match; and, even if one is not measuring oneself against a more powerful neighbour, it is human to be exhilarated by the acquisition and exercise of greater power than one has hitherto possessed—and this even when the power in question is of a merely material kind. Here we have an explanation of the present-day sanctification of the word 'science'. Science, married to technology, has generated material power; this material power has been forged into potent weapons; and the desire, partly rational and partly irrational, to possess these weapons stimulates a desire to master the science to which the weapons manifestly owe their origin.

The sanctification of the word 'democracy' is not so easy to understand. The immediate explanation of it is, no doubt, to be found in the prestige of those West European peoples whose colonial empires recently extended over so large a part of Asia and Africa. The Asian and African peoples disliked Western rule, of course, and they have been unexpectedly successful in getting rid of it in double-quick time since the West

itself gave them the opportunity by inflicting the Second
World War on itself. Yet, while the non-Western subject
peoples jibbed against Western rule, they were impressed
by the power that enabled a small Western country to
conquer and hold down a non-Western sub-continent.
The subjects, or ex-subjects, of the former West
European colonial powers have sought to read the secret
of their former rulers' strength in the hope of tapping
the source of this strength for their own benefit. In the
last chapter of the history of Western colonialism the
leading West European colonial powers were France,
Britain, the Netherlands, and Belgium. By the time they
had acquired their colonial empires overseas, all these
four West European countries had taken to governing
themselves at home by parliamentary regimes with a
wide franchise on the home front, and they stood for
'democracy' in this usage of the word though they did
not stand for it on the colonial front till the end of the
colonial story. Meanwhile, these leading West European
colonial powers were simultaneously democratic at home
and powerful overseas; and their Asian and African temporary subjects consequently constructed a syllogism
which Aristotle would certainly have disallowed as being
illogical. 'The West European peoples live under democratic political regimes; the West European peoples are
powerful; therefore democracy is a source of power;
therefore we Asians and Africans must become democratic as well as scientific if we are to attain our objective
of getting even with the West in the competition for
power and for the advantages that power brings with
it.'

This argument is obviously unsound. In fact, its mode
of thought is not logical but magical. At the same time
there may be a logical connection between Western
democracy and Western power, though this will be a
different one from the connection that Asian and African
minds have imagined. The truth perhaps is that democracy, so far from having been one of the sources of the
Western peoples' power, has been one of the luxuries
that their power has enabled them to afford. The source
of their power has been their marriage of technology
with science; the opportunity for their democracy has
been the margin of strength, wealth, and security which
their power, derived from applied science, has created
for them. Democracy is an attractive regime for the
majority—and this is a vast majority in any country—
that is subject to the government without having a hand
in the government. A democratic regime gives this
majority a modicum of control over the government that
is genuine, and it also gives them the comforting illusion
of enjoying a great deal more control than they ever
succeed in exercising in reality. This is a political luxury,
but it is one that cannot be indulged in unless one
possesses a margin of security, wealth, and power within
which one can play the fool with impunity. Democratic
parliamentary government is a less efficient, and therefore a more wasteful, regime than oligarchic parliamentary government, and even a parliamentary oligarchy is
inefficient and extravagant by comparison with a well-
managed authoritarian regime. Parliamentary government and, *a fortiori,* parliamentary government with a
wide franchise, is a political extravagance that is a

political hall-mark of already achieved power, wealth, and security. It is a tax on these assets; it is not one of their sources. Unlike the belief that science has been a source of Western power, the belief that democracy has been a source of Western power is a fallacy. Democracy had been a Western amenity that Western power has brought within the West's reach.

There is, all the same, one genuine point of resemblance between the non-Western World's pursuit of democracy and its pursuit of science. It seems evident, sad though this is, that, in both cases, the pursuit is not disinterested. The non-Western peoples are not cultivating democracy and science for their own sakes. They are not attracted towards them by a recognition of intrinsic merits in them. The attraction lies in the real or fancied efficacy of science and democracy as talismans for imparting to the non-Western majority the power that has given the Western minority its temporary ascendancy.

The majority has suffered so much from this ascendancy, and has resented it so keenly, that it might have been expected to sheer away from the West if and when it had recovered its freedom to do so. It has actually recovered this freedom of choice in the act of recovering its political independence, but it has not, in fact, taken the line that its experience and its feelings might have led an observer to prophesy before the event. He might reasonably have prophesied that a politically liberated non-Western country would voluntarily appropriate only those elements in the Western way of life that it believed, whether rightly or wrongly, to be the springs of Western power. It would decide to appropriate these, even if it found them intrinsically distasteful. It would make them its own nevertheless, because bitter experience would have driven home the lesson that the mastery of Western weapons was the only alternative to falling under the West's ascendancy. But the liberated non-Western country, so it might have been forecast, would have limited its borrowings from the Western way of life to this indispensable minimum. Apart from that, it would have used its recovered liberty for the reactionary purpose of jumping clear of the West. It would have sought, as far as possible, to return to its own traditional way of life that it used to follow in the days before the West crossed its path.

This forecast would have been reasonable, but, as we now know, it would have been wide of the mark. So far, at any rate, the non-Western peoples have used their recovered political freedom not to repudiate the Western way of life, but to embrace it. And this is really not so surprising as it might seem at first sight. Part of the explanation of this voluntary continuation of the process of Westernization is to be found in the nature of the class of people that has come to the top in the new independent regimes in the liberated countries. The political rewards have naturally gone to those people who bore the brunt of the political struggle for independence. This battle had to be fought with Western weapons in the most comprehensive usage of the word—a usage that includes not only physical weapons of war but all kinds of immaterial things, such as tactics, strategy, policies, and, above all, ideas and ideals. These Western weapons could and did win the political battle for the non-Western party to the conflict. But the price of political victory was spiritual captivation. The non-Western men and women who defeated the West by fighting the West with Western weapons became spiritually enthralled, in the process, by the Western way of life. Involuntarily they became exemplars and exponents of voluntary self-Westernization; and, when they found themselves in the saddle as a result of their political success, they took it for granted that, for a liberated non-Western country, the purpose of self-liberation from Western rule was to enter the community of nations leading the Western way of life. They would not, of course, label this way 'Western'; they would label it 'modern'; but 'Western' would be what they would mean. They would mean the way of life that they had made their own in the course of their political struggle. Now that they were in power, they would use their power for completing the trans-position of their country's traditional way of life into a 'modern', i.e. a Western, mode.

The West can fairly congratulate itself on this captiva-tion of Asian and African nationalists by the Western way of life. For this is evidence that these opponents of Western political ascendancy have found something in the Western Civilization that seems to them to be in-trinsically valuable. They would not have been capti-vated if they had found there nothing that was of value to them except as a means to another end—as a means, that is to say, towards getting their fingers upon the Western levers of power. What, then, are the elements in the Western way of life that non-Westerners have found attractive on their own merits and for their own sakes? The Western spiritual commodity that has been found attractive intrinsically is, I believe, neither democracy nor science but social justice.

In the days when the Western colonial powers were reluctantly yielding to their non-Western subjects' demands for independence, Western die-hards used to call for the maintenance of Western rule on the ground that this offered the only hope of social justice for the non-Western masses. They claimed, with truth, that Western colonial rule had done something at least to mitigate an age-old native regime of extreme inequality and oppression. The Western die-hards prophesied that, if the Western colonial administrators abdicated, the old native oppressors of the poor would return to power and would resume their traditional malpractices; and then the masses would sink back into their miserable pre-colonial plight. This forecast was not insincere, though, of course, it was also not disinterested. But the significant point about it is that it has been proved totally mistaken by the actual subsequent course of events. The former Western colonial administrators have been replaced, not by their predecessors and subsequent protégés the traditional rulers, but by their pupils and eventual opponents the leaders of the movements for independence. These post-colonial national rulers have promptly deprived the traditional native rulers of the last shreds of their power and wealth, and have eagerly introduced the post-second-world-war Western welfare state into the liberated Asian and African countries. Foreign rulers find it advisable to be wary of taking political action that damages native vested interests or touches the intimate side of the native population's private life. Their hold over their native subjects is too precarious to warrant their taking such risks as these. A national regime need not have these inhibitions; and the Western colonial administrators' successors have certainly not had them. They have been boldly carrying out radical measures that their foreign predecessors would not have dared even to contemplate. They have been redistributing the land, emancipating the women, imposing steeply graduated taxation on the rich, and even assailing such ancient and strongly entrenched institutions as caste. And their inspiration, in this campaign of benevolent iconoclasm, has been the present-day Western ideal of social justice.

This movement has been initiated by a small, though powerful, Western-educated minority, but the ferment is already working its way through the masses. For the first time since the dawn of civilization about five thousand years ago, the masses have now become alive to the possibility that their traditional way of life might be changed for the better and that this change might be brought about by their own action. This awakening of hope and purpose in the hearts and minds of the hitherto depressed three-quarters of the World's population will, I feel certain, stand out in retrospect as the epoch-making event of our age. The tapping of atomic energy and its application to the forging of weapons and to the exploration of outer space will be seen to have been trifles by comparison. As for the present-day conflict between competing ideologies, this will, I should guess, be as meaningless to our descendants, three hundred years from now, as our sixteenth-century and seventeenth-century Western ancestors' wars of religion already are to us. On the other hand the emancipation of the World's women and industrial workers and peasants will, I believe, loom larger and larger; and, so far as this stands to the Western Civilization's credit, this Western Civilization will receive, and deserve, the blessing of posterity.

The West can legitimately claim substantial credit, for it has not only conceived the ideal of social justice; it has also conjured up the material means for translating this ideal into practice. During the millennia before the modern Western marriage of technology with science, the surplus produced by society, beyond what was required for bare subsistence, was so small that it sufficed only to give a privileged minority a share in the amenities of civilization. The modern Western increase in productivity through the application of science has been so enormous that it can now give the same amenities to the whole of mankind—unless, of course, we use our new material power for committing mass-suicide.

The ideal of equality for women with men and for industrial workers and peasants with bourgeois and aristocrats is of recent origin even in the West. Even here it has not been put into practice till within the life-time of people who are still alive. But these secular applications in the West of the ideal of social justice have not been the first. The earliest expression of this ideal was the demand that there should be equality for dis-senters with the orthodox, whatever the local orthodoxy

might happen to be, and this demand dates from before
the end of the seventeenth century. The introduction of
religious toleration in the West was contemporaneous
with the marriage between technology and science there,
and this synchronicity was not accidental. The application of toleration to religion and of science to technology
were two different reactions against an identical evil,
namely the destructiveness and wickedness of the
Western wars of religion.

The ideal of social justice, as well as the pursuit of
science, has, as we have seen, been taken over from the
West by the new regimes that have been replacing the
West European colonial empires in Asia and Africa. On
the other hand, the West's traditional religion has not
proved anything like so attractive to the non-Western
majority of the human race; and in this important point
the World's reaction to the impact of the West has been
the same as its previous reaction to the impact of
Hellenism. In either case the World has been impressed
and influenced, at least for a time, by a number of
secular elements in a dominant society's way of life, but
in both cases the dominant society's religion has left the
rest of the human race cold. You remember the sequel
in the Hellenic case. The sequel was a counter-offensive
on the spiritual plane which ended in the conversion
of the dominant society to religions that had originated among its native subjects. History, I suggested
in that context, is not bound to repeat itself but also
is not bound not to; so the last act of the Ancient
Greek drama reveals to us one of the alternative possible denouements of the Western drama that is still

in course of being played on the stage of the present-day world.

Why has Western Christianity been less successful than Western science, democracy, and social justice in winning the allegiance of the non-Western majority of mankind? I am not, I think, under-estimating Western Christianity's success outside the Western World's own bounds. Western missionaries have carried Roman Catholic and Protestant Christianity to the ends of the Earth, and in our own day the political emancipation of the West's former Asian and African subjects has had its ecclesiastical counterpart. The Western missionaries have been handing over to their converts the leadership of the convert Christian communities. The Asian and African Protestant churches have become self-governing; the Asian and African Roman Catholic communities could not achieve that without ceasing to be Catholic; but the local representatives of the hierachy are now being recruited more and more from the local converts, and this liberal policy has been adopted by the Vatican on its own initiative, I believe. Yet the non-Western converts to Roman Catholicism and to Protestantism are, and seem likely to continue to be, no more than an infinitesimally small fraction of the great non-Western majority of the human race. So the relative unpopularity of Western religion, by comparison with the relative popularity of a number of the secular elements in the Western way of life, does raise a question that calls for an answer.

Part of the answer might take the form of another question: Why has the West's ancestral religion been

losing ground progressively in the West itself within
these last three hundred years? The elements in Christianity, whatever these may be, that have proved
stumbling-blocks for modern Westerners may be the
elements that have also made Christianity unattractive
to the non-Western World. One of the stumbling-blocks
in Christianity for modern Western minds has been an
intellectual one. Some of the traditional tenets of Christianity are incompatible with some of the findings of
modern Western science. A greater stumbling-block has
been a moral one. The early modern Western wars of
religion, and the atrocities that unhappily accompanied
them, were ugly manifestations of an intolerant vein in
Christianity; and this same vein had burst out in the
same ugly way on more than one previous occasion. In
the seventeenth-century Western World this aspect of
the West's ancestral Christianity gave Western hearts a
shock that has left its mark in a permanent sense of
alienation; and, with the passage of time, this negative
attitude towards the West's ancestral religion has been
spreading to wider and wider circles within the Western
Society.

Christianity is one member of a group of religions
which have all occasionally been betrayed into atrocious-
ness by intolerance, and this, I think, for an identical
reason. Christianity, Islam, and Judaism all have the
same picture of God, and it is a picture that presents
two facets which have never yet been reconciled. These
religions all see God as being loving, compassionate, and
merciful; but they also see the same God as being jealous,
wrathful, and vindictive. The belief in God's jealousy

leads a believer to believe that his own particular religion, or even his own particular sect of it, is God's exclusive revelation, and that therefore the Church, or the practice of the church, that has received this revelation holds a monopoly of the truth and of the means of salvation. On the other hand, the belief in God's loving-kindness leads a believer to believe that God is the father of all men and that He will not have left any of His children utterly in the dark. In all the religions in this group there is an unresolved conflict between the two attitudes of mind and rules of conduct which the two incompatible pictures of God inspire. And in the modern secular ideologies of Jewish and Christian origin the two warring spirits re-appear. The ideal of Liberalism is a secular expression of Jewish and Christian charity; the ideal of Nationalism is a secular expression of Jewish and Christian exclusiveness and intolerance. In the doctrine of Communism an intense concern for social justice, which is Communism's original driving force, is combined with a belief that the industrial proletariat is History's exclusively chosen people. This combination of elements in Communism is incongruous, but it is the same incongruity as that which manifests itself in Communism's parent religions.

The intolerant vein in the religions in the Jewish-Christian-Muslim group has produced shocking and devastating atrocities in the past. I am thinking here of the forcible suppression of the practice of all non-Christian religions in the Christian Roman Empire towards the end of the fourth century of the Christian Era; I am also thinking of the Muslim jihads and of the

Christian crusades, as well as of the fratricidal Western
Christian wars between Roman Catholics and Protes-
tants in the Early Modern Age. These atrocities that have
been committed up to date in the names of the religions
in this group have been as wicked as they could be; but
fortunately they have not also been as devastating as
they could be in their material effects. They could and
would have been far more devastating if they had been
committed at some date since science has been putting
itself at the disposal of technology for the forging of
more and more lethal weapons. They would be almost
inconceivably devastating if they were ever to break out
again in the Atomic Age upon which the World has
now been launched by the West.

The sinfulness of sin is, of course, intrinsic, and perhaps this was what President Coolidge was trying to
convey in his celebrated comment on sin that he was
'against it'. Grievous sins are frequently committed without bringing penalties upon the sinner's head, at least
in this life. There are also situations in which 'the wages
of sin is death' in the literal sense of death in this world.
These variations in the immediate consequences of sin
are morally meaningless. They are consequences of
variations in non-moral factors in human life—technological factors in the case in point. Yet conscience is not
so strong a spiritual force that it can afford to disdain
reinforcement by baser considerations such as, for instance, the impulse towards self-preservation. In any case,
this impulse seems bound, in the Atomic Age, to exert
a powerful, and perhaps even a decisive, influence on
people's attitudes, choices, and actions. It is already

being recognized that, in this age, there is one particular
choice, and this an extreme one, that confronts the whole
human race. We have either to resign ourselves to committing mass-suicide or else to learn to live together as a
single family. This second alternative, which is the only
alternative to self-annihilation, requires the abolition of
the existing barriers between different races, nations,
religions, and ideologies. There will therefore be a
premium on ideals, ideas, and institutions that make for
unity, concord, and love; and conversely, those that make
[for discord] and hatred will incur odium. This,
[indeed, is the touc]hstone on which all the existing
[ideologi]es are going to be assayed by the
[Ato]mic Age; and the ideologies' and
[religions' reaction to] this test will decide whether they
[are to be accepte]d or to be rejected.

[Exc]lusive-mindedness and intolerance
[will ...]ut out of court any religion or
[ideology ...] with these deadly vices and that
[...] them. And this is surely going to
[...] religions in the Jewish-Christian-
[...] some of the ideologies that have
[... n]ationalism and Communism, for
[... argu]ed that Judaism and Christianity
[... Comm]unism as well, have another side
which is incompatible with their intolerance and ex-
clusive-mindedness; and it is conceivable that their bright
side might at last prevail over their dark side now that
the wages of this sinful vein in them have been raised to
a prohibitive magnitude by Western technology's recent
feat of tapping atomic energy. It is not only conceivable

Handwritten marginalia:
Ten sex drive / reeds forever. / www.lp.org / Aquinas & Augustine: / GOOD WHORE'S LEGAL. / VOTE LIBERTARIAN / www.legalbrothels.com

but is, I believe, certain that the three South-West-Asian religions will now have to make the choice between those two veins in them which, as I see it, are morally incompatible with each other. To my mind, this is the most important single issue now confronting the West and the World as a whole. This issue concerns the whole World, because the West's choice between charity and intolerance in the field of religion seems likely to have a decisive influence on the World's future attitude towards the Western Civilization.

Whatever may be the future of the religions and ideologies in this South-West-Asian group, the human race as a whole is not committed to them. We have a choice; for half the human race today adheres to religions and philosophies that have originated, not in South-West Asia, but in India and China. Buddhism and Hinduism, between them, bestride half the World, and in Eastern Asia Confucianism may still re-emerge from its present eclipse. This eastern group of religions and philosophies will, of course, be required to stand the Atomic-Age test, and Hinduism will not emerge from this with a clean charge-sheet. The high-caste Hindus share with the speakers of three Teutonic languages— English, Dutch, and German—the odious distinction of practising 'apartheid'; and racialism is a form of exclusiveness that is surely going to be condemned by all but the tiny offending fraction of mankind. However, Buddhism, in contrast to Hinduism, has always ignored caste-distinctions. And, when we pass from the plane of social practice to the plane of intellectual outlook, Hinduism, too, comes out well by comparison with the

religions and ideologies of the South-West-Asian group.
In contrast to these, Hinduism has the same outlook as
the pre-Christian and pre-Muslim religions and philosophies of the western half of the Old World. Like
them, Hinduism takes it for granted that there is more
than one valid approach to truth and to salvation, and
that these different approaches are not only compatible
with each other but are complementary.

Hinduism's intellectual tolerance makes Hinduism *par
excellence* a candidate for serving as the religion of co-
existence; co-existence is mankind's only alternative to
mass-suicide in the Atomic Age; and mankind means to
save itself from committing mass-suicide if it can find
a way. One open way is the Indian way; and it might
therefore seem probable that, in the Atomic Age, the
spirit of Indian religion and philosophy will receive a
welcome in the western half of the World. In opening
their minds and hearts to this spirit, the Jewish-Christian-
Muslim half of the human race would be reopening
them to the spirit of the tolerant religions and philosophies that were their ancestors' guiding lights in the
days before Judaism, Christianity and Islam made their
appearance.

But they would be doing something more positive and
significant than that. They would be making a whole-
hearted and decisive choice in favour of the spirit of
love in their own religious tradition. The Jewish-Christian-Muslim picture of God as being merciful, compassionate, loving, and self-sacrificing is, I would again
suggest, incompatible with the picture of God as being
jealous, wrathful, and vindictive. But it is complemen-

tary to the Indian spirit of tolerance. Is it too much to hope that, in the great spiritual crisis through which we are living in our time, the World's two great religious traditions may work together to save mankind from destroying itself?

III

PARLIAMENTARY DEMOCRACY
ON TRIAL

I N the preceding chapter I noted that the Western institution of parliamentary democracy has been proving attractive to the non-Western majority of mankind, and I discussed some of the possible reasons for this. Whatever the reasons, there can be no doubt about the fact. It is true that, among the countries which, in our time, have been liberated from authoritarian rule, native or foreign, a number have quickly fallen under authoritarian rule again. Nearly all of these new authoritarian regimes belong to one or other of two classes. They are either Communist regimes or regimes of the Cromwellian type in which the Army has ousted the politicians and has replaced them by major-generals. But it is also true, I believe, that there is not a single case in which a regime of either of these two kinds has been a liberated country's first choice. Invariably its first choice has been Western parliamentary democracy, and it has been only if and when parliamentary democracy has obviously failed to answer to the occasion that it has been discarded in favour of either Communism or Army government. It is surely significant that parliamentary democracy was the first choice in both Russia and China, which are the two leading Communist countries today.

In Russia the immediate cause of the overthrow of the Czardom was Russia's failure to hold her own against Germany in the First World War. By the date of this first of the two Russian revolutions in the year 1917, Russia's domestic life was disorganized and her military effort was already near breaking-point. There could hardly have been a more adverse setting than this for the inauguration of a new regime, and it is neither surprising in itself nor a reflection on the Russian people's political capacity that the regime that was launched in these untoward circumstances should have failed to keep afloat for more than a few months. What is remarkable is that the regime which was the Russians' first choice in 1917 was Western parliamentary democracy. Lenin did not get his chance to make the second Russian revolution of 1917 and to introduce Bolshevik socialism (later relabelled 'Communism') until Kerensky had been given his chance to try to make parliamentary democracy achieve the impossible. Kerensky's assignment was to carry on the war and to restore order in the interior of the country. It was a foregone conclusion that no regime could achieve both these objectives simultaneously. The Bolsheviks had the strength of mind to make peace with Germany on cruelly hard terms, and even then it took them several years to make their authority at home effective—partly, of course, because their Russian opponents received military support from some of the victorious Western powers that were Russia's ex-allies. The Bolsheviks' eventual success suggests that Kerensky's attempt to carry on the war may have been Kerensky's fatal mistake, but this was a mistake in the field of foreign policy, and it might have been made by a regime of any ideological complexion. It does not prove that a parliamentary regime was unsuitable for early-twentieth-century Russia intrinsically. No doubt, it may have been. This is a question to which we shall have to return. But the desperate plight into which Russia had already fallen in 1917 before Kerensky's parliamentary democratic regime was installed would be enough to account for the shortness of this regime's life.

In China the would-be parliamentary democratic regime of the Kuomintang started life under less appalling conditions. It is true that the Kuomintang had to conquer its hold upon China by force of arms, and this in a war on two fronts against the Chinese war-lords and the Chinese Communists. But Chiang Kai-shek, unlike Kerensky, did not have a foreign war on his hands until after he had won—or, at least, temporarily won—the civil war in China. By 1929 the Kuomintang had re-united, under its own rule, the whole of China, including even Manchuria nominally. And the Chinese people gave the Kuomintang twenty years' grace, reckoning from 1929, for trying to make parliamentary democracy a working reality in China before they acquiesced in its replacement by the Communist regime that was the alternative choice. During the greater part of that twenty years' period, the Kuomintang was, of course, severely handicapped. Its suppression of the Chinese Communists in 1927 had been only partially effective, and, from that date till the Communists' effective suppression of the

Kuomintang in 1948-9, Chiang Kai-shek never managed either to liquidate the Communists completely or to come to terms with them satisfactorily. At the same time, China had to face Japanese aggression from 1931 to 1945. Chiang Kai-shek's handicaps during his twenty years were, in fact, only less severe than Kerensky's handicaps had been during his few months. All the same, parliamentary democracy did have thirty or forty times as long a trial in China as it had in Russia, and the Kuomintang cannot be judged as leniently as Kerensky is entitled to be judged when we are trying to assess the causes of parliamentary democracy's failure. The Kuomintang, during their twenty years, never came as near as Kerensky had come to establishing parliamentary democracy in reality as well as in name. All the same, there can be no doubt that the Kuomintang's founding father, Sun Yat-sen, was sincere in making parliamentary democracy the party's ultimate objective. There can be no doubt, either, that he showed common sense in planning to approach this objective by stages. Since the Chinese people gave the Kuomintang twenty years' grace before they allowed themselves to become completely disillusioned with it, there can be little doubt, again, that the parliamentary democracy which was the Kuomintang's professed objective was also the Chinese people's first choice as a modern substitute for the venerable but effete imperial regime.

If parliamentary democracy really was the Russian and the Chinese peoples' first choice, and if their choices were typical of the preference of a majority of the liberated countries, why is it that parliamentary democracy has failed to hold the field in one liberated country after another? Perhaps we can find the clue to an answer if we glance at the history, up to date, of the sequel to liberation in India. India has been exceptional among non-Western countries in having made a decided success of parliamentary democracy so far; and her success in this undertaking is an important fact, considering that India is one of the two countries that have the largest areas and populations, and the oldest surviving civilizations, in all Asia.

If one is travelling in Asia and enters India after having visited some of the other South Asian countries, one becomes conscious of a difference in human climate. This can be expressed in numerical terms. In India one meets a large number of people who are obviously able, experienced, responsible, and public-spirited citizens. One meets them in many different walks of life, not only in politics but in government service, in the universities, in the press, in business. India has suceeded in building up this fund of good citizens thanks to the promptness of the Hindus, in the early stages of their encounter with the Western World, in appropriating some of the key elements of the Western Civilization. Thus India has started out on her career as an independent state in the community of modern nations comparatively well equipped with the personnel that is indispensable for making parliamentary democracy work.

The word 'comparatively' cannot be omitted; for no would-be democratic state anywhere, either in the East or in the West, has ever yet been adequately staffed with citizens of the necessary kind. That is why parliamentary democracy's performance has so far been lamentably imperfect, even in those countries in which it originated and in which it is therefore presumably best adapted to the local social setting. India's equipment for operating a parliamentary democratic regime is comparatively good, and her performance, so far, has been correspondingly impressive. Here is a country with a vast area, with a great and growing population, with the narrowest margin of production over the requirements of bare subsistence, with a low percentage of literacy, and with an experience of parliamentary government that was only thirty years old in 1947—the year in which India's independence was achieved. There has never before been an electorate on the Indian scale; yet general elections in India appear to be efficiently organized and honestly conducted. The polling is heavy; the public interest in the political issues is keen. The practical difficulties arising from illiteracy have been surmounted by ingenious polling devices. In present-day India, parliamentary democracy is a reality. This is greatly to the credit of the Indian people as a whole, but even greater credit is due to the modern-minded minority in India that has been serving the country as a political leaven.

The success of parliamentary democracy in India stands out in contrast to its failure, on first trial, in Pakistan. The difference is not easy to account for adequately. The Pakistanis and the Indians are inhabitants of the same sub-continent. They were exposed to the same Western influences under the same Western colonial regime. They entered on their careers as independent states at the same date. The difference in the political out-

come in the first chapter of the story is perhaps a consequence of the difference in the respective reactions of
Hindus and Indian Muslims to the impact of the West
over a preceding period of nearly two hundred years,
beginning with the establishment of the British East
India Company's rule over Bengal. The history of these
antecedents of India's and Pakistan's simultaneous
attainment of independence in 1947 is too long to be re-
capitulated in the present context. The sequel to the
breakdown of the first attempt at parliamentary democracy in Pakistan has a more immediate bearing on the
subject of this chapter.

Some of the deposed Pakistani politicians, and also
some Pakistani business men who were associated with
them, have been accused of malpractices by the regime
that has taken their place, These charges, coming from
this quarter, can hardly be quite disinterested. At the
same time they can hardly be quite untrue; for, if they
were, the ignominious dismissal of the politicians would
not have been acquiesced in by the people—as it has
been even by a minority that also disapproves of and dis-
likes the regime that has now stepped into the previous
regime's shoes. This new regime is a military one, and
that was virtually inevitable, since in Pakistan there was
no local Communist movement capable of taking advantage of the professedly democratic politicians' fiasco.
The replacement of a parliamentary democratic regime
in Pakistan by a military regime is more or less common
form in the history of an ex-colonial Asian country. The
unusual and encouraging feature in Pakistan's case is
that President Ayub and his colleagues have rather

quickly introduced a new constitution that is designed
eventually to make their own military regime superfluous.

The intention embodied in this new constitution is to
give the people of Pakistan the means of educating themselves in the art of operating democracy. The method is
to give them practice in this on a small scale and at a
low level to begin with. The declared ultimate aim is to
re-establish parliamentary democracy in Pakistan, but
this only after the people have acquired enough political
experience and sufficient sense of political responsibility
to give a parliamentary democratic regime a chance of
working effectively and honestly at a second attempt. I
believe that the present government of Pakistan sincerely
intends to carry out its declared programme. Of course
their plan may miscarry. The political enterprise on
which they have embarked is one that is obviously difficult to accomplish. Yet, if their professed intentions are
genuine, as I believe they are, their experiment is one
that is of very great general interest, and this whether it
succeeds or whether it fails. Even if this experiment is
only partially successful, it will have been an instructive
piece of political pioneering. Its notable merit is that it
faces the difficulties inherent in parliamentary democracy and introduces constructive measures for trying to
overcome them.

The new constitution of Pakistan has been labelled
'basic democracy' by its author, President Ayub. This
label is not self-explanatory, but the key to the interpre-
tation of it is, I believe, the older term 'basic English'.
Democracy in Pakistan is, at the present stage, to be

'basic' in the sense that it is to be stripped down to its naked essence—the minimum below which it would be impossible to reduce democracy without changing it into something that would no longer answer to the name. What is this minimum? In President Ayub's view, as mirrored in his new constitution, it is the democratic control of parish affairs by the parishioners themselves. This means, in effect, the election of parish councils, and also the election of electors who are to represent their parishes in the election of members of provincial councils, and so on, tier above tier, till we arrive at the indirect election of a national parliament. The political experience gained by the primary electors on a small scale may eventually qualify them to cope with public affairs on a larger scale; and, if and when this stage of political education is reached, the scaffolding now interposed between the primary electors and the national parliament can presumably be removed. When this happens, the device of indirect election will have been eliminated from the constitution, and the primary electorate will then vote direct at all levels of the constitutional structure, up to the highest.

Indirect election! Electoral colleges! This is the anatomy of President Ayub's 'basic democracy', and now we know where we are; for this is also the anatomy of the constitutions of the Soviet Union and the United States. It is reassuring to find that 'basic democracy' in Pakistan is not a leap in the dark, but is a variation on an expedient that has been tried more than once before. The repeated recurrence to this expedient suggests that there must be a good reason for it, and that this reason must be founded on something basic in human nature, considering that constitutions of this pyramidal kind have been installed in a number of different countries over a period that, by now, has run to about a hundred and seventy years.

The provisions in the Constitution of the United States for the creation of the President are akin, in principle, to President Ayub's 'basic democracy'. The powers of the primary electors are limited to the election of an electoral college. The election of the President is placed in this college's hands. The original letter of the American Constitution still stands today, with the device now labelled 'basic democracy' written into it. The American primary electors have, of course, long since circumvented the founding fathers' constrictive device. They have respected the letter but have overridden the spirit. They have reduced the institutional functions of the electoral college to nullity by binding over the members of the college in advance, as a condition of their being elected, to execute a mandate that the primary electors have imposed upon them. If the parties respected the spirit as well as the letter of the Constitution, the members of the electoral college, as well as the primary electors, would recognize it to be their constitutional duty to elect the candidate who was the best in their judgement. Actually, the electoral college was turned long ago into a superfluous cog in the wheel of electoral procedure, and this virtual elimination of the electoral college is by now such ancient history that, in a normal election, the very existence of the electoral college is forgotten. A combination of unusual circumstances brought the college to light for a moment in the course of the Presidential election of

1960; and the electorate was then amazed and amused to learn that, on this occasion, the electoral college might prove to be something more than a cipher.

Probably the general verdict today would be that 'basic democracy' is a transitory phase in the very nature of things, even if it is conceded that in some cases this may have been a necessary stage in an electorate's political education. It will be pointed out that the American electorate quickly attained to a degree of political maturity at which it became qualified, *de facto*, to elect the President of the United States direct, and that it then made its own arrangements for circumventing those provisions in the Constitution by which the founding fathers had sought to keep the primary electors' functions within 'basic' limits. The long-since self-emancipated American electors will by now probably be willing to make the handsome gesture of agreeing that the degree of maturity which they themselves reached yesterday is likely to be reached by younger electorates tomorrow. It will then be concluded that 'basic democracy' is destined eventually to be eliminated in Pakistan as it has already been eliminated in the United States.

This train of reasoning rests on the calculation that any electorate will make progress in acquiring political capacity through being given the opportunity of learning by experience. But in this calculation there is one assumption that has not been borne out by the course of human affairs since the date on which the Constitution of the United States was brought into force. This assumption is that, while electorates will be achieving cumulative increases of political knowledge, the amount of things to be known in the field of politics, and the facilities for knowing these things, will have continued to remain constant. It is true that knowledge has been increasing and is likely to increase still further. But it is also true that the amount of things to be known has also increased, that this has increased out of all proportion to the electorate's increase in knowledge, and that to obtain knowledge that is relevant to political action has also been becoming more and more difficult.

The application of democracy to the parliamentary system of government is a relatively recent innovation. There is no intrinsic or necessary connection between the parliamentary system and a wide franchise; and, in fact, this system has been associated not with democracy but with oligarchy during the greater part of its history up to date. The earliest moves to extend the franchise were those made in the Constitution of the United States, in some of the numerous successive constitutions of Revolutionary France, and in the British Reform Bill of 1832. Even after the process had been started, it was carried out in instalments. Universal adult suffrage for both sexes is an event of our own life-time. The new departure of extending the franchise, even to a minimum degree, implies an assumption. This assumption is that public affairs are simple enough to be understood and handled by the electorate of the day, whatever the extent of the franchise may be at the moment. The statesmen who first introduced democracy into the parliamentary system of government did undoubtedly believe that public affairs were sufficiently simple to warrant their extending the franchise. At the same time, they took, as we have noticed, the precaution of keeping democracy within 'basic' limits where it was a question of voting on the highest issues, and they were also wary of giving the franchise to layers of the population which, in their judgement, would be incapable of dealing effectively and responsibly even with such simple things as public affairs and even within 'basic' limits.

If we take the date of the coming into force of the American Constitution as marking the beginning of the application of democracy to the parliamentary system of government, we can see that, in the course of the hundred and seventy years that have elapsed since then, there have been two simultaneous developments which, between them, have falsified the founding fathers' sober expectations and have perhaps even undermined the foundations of their constitutional edifice. On the one hand the franchise in most parliamentary states has been widened progressively till it has arrived at universal adult suffrage. At the same time, public affairs have not grown progressively simpler, as they should have done if the progressive extension of the franchise to more and more callow strata of the population was to be justifiable on the founding fathers' criterion. On the contrary, public affairs have been growing progressively more complicated and more inscrutable, till, in the present era of universal adult suffrage, these affairs have come to be beyond the comprehension not only of the electors but even of the electors' elected representatives, and perhaps even of the members of the government itself.

Moreover, this increasing complication of public affairs is not a piece of wanton sabotage. It is not, for instance, just a product of the perverse pedantry of a growing host of public servants. The reason why public servants have now become legion is identical with the reason why public affairs have become complicated. The growing complexity of public affairs is a consequence, and an inescapable one, of the growing complexity of human affairs in general. These have been made increasingly complicated by the increasing progress of technology; this technological advance got up steam in the Industrial Revolution in Britain; and the Industrial Revolution in Britain was contemporaneous with the political revolution in America. During these last hundred and seventy years the tendencies on the economic and on the political plane have not been in harmony with each other; they have been at odds. As a result, we have arrived simultaneously at universal adult suffrage and at a state of public affairs in which these have become a mystery—or, rather, a whole labyrinth of mysteries—which no one but a handful of whole-time professional experts is able any longer to understand, administer, or control.

This point is illustrated by two examples from the recent history of democracy in the United Kingdom. The objective of democracy is to give the people the maximum possible amount of control over the government; and, for this purpose, there were two institutions in nineteenth-century British public life that were of outstanding importance. One of these was the parliamentary question; the other was the administration of the income-tax by Commissioners of Inland Revenue who were the representatives, not of the Government, but of the tax-payers themselves. Both institutions were designed to keep under control not so much the Government, perhaps, as the corps of professional public servants who conduct the administration of the country on the Government's behalf. This common intention of both institutions has now, however, been largely frustrated by the growing complexity of public affairs. A member of parliament still possesses, unimpaired, his constitutional right to put questions to the Government and to receive prompt and honest answers. Questions are still put, and the answers are certainly still as prompt, and, I am sure, also still as honest, as they ever were. But, as an instrument for democratic control, the parliamentary question has nevertheless been becoming less and less effective. The reason is that it has been becoming more and more difficult for a member of parliament to acquire the knowledge and information needed for discerning what is the pertinent question to ask and what is the telling way of framing it. As for the United Kingdom income-tax, I very much doubt whether the Commissioners are any longer *au fait* with the laws and regulations governing its administration, and I know that the tax-payers themselves are not. The only people who are still able to keep abreast of the necessary knowledge are full-time professional experts. On the government side there are the parliamentary draftsmen who work out the finance bills and the inspectors and collectors of income-tax who administer the law. The tax-payer, on his side, has to employ private experts to parley with the Government's experts. The tax-payer pays whatever sums his own experts tell him that they have agreed on his behalf with their official opposite numbers. The twentieth-century

British tax-payer finds himself in the position of the nineteenth-century native. 'As a sheep, before her shearers', he is 'dumb'.

These are, I think, two fair samples of what has been happening over the whole field of public affairs in all democratic parliamentary countries, including those in which both parliamentary government and a wide franchise are of the oldest standing. The upshot is that, even in the countries in which the democratic parliamentary system of government is today comparatively well-seasoned and mature, democracy is being reduced, in effect, nearer and nearer to a 'basic' level. This whittling away of the citizen's control over the Government has not been due to any deliberate action on the part of the public servants; it has been due to the operation of a force that is impersonal and inexorable. The effective working of full democracy is being defeated by the increasing complication of affairs under the impulsion of technology.

If the foregoing analysis is correct, parliamentary democracy is on trial today not only in Pakistan and in other recently liberated Asian and African countries. It is on trial in every country in the World in which parliamentary democracy of some kind is the officially established regime or the officially designated goal of constitutional development.

Up to this point we have been looking at what has been happening to parliamentary democracy within the framework of one or other of the World's local states. There are now a hundred or more of these, and, between them, they embrace the whole inhabited part of the

Earth's surface and the whole living generation of the human race. Obviously the domestic politics of these local states are a matter of great concern to mankind. At the same time there is another plane of the present-day world's political life that is of still greater concern to us all, and that is the plane of present-day international relations and of a possible future world-government. What happens inside each of the World's hundred national states will merely decrease, or alternatively increase, mankind's well-being and happiness. What happens on the international plane is a matter of life and death for the human race; and, on this crucial plane of public affairs, democracy is still in its infancy.

If we avoid committing mass-suicide, there is no reason why we should not eventually be able to have a world-state with a democratic parliamentary constitution. But, if we *are* to avoid mass-suicide, we must have our world-state quickly, and this probably means that we must have it in a non-democratic constitutional form to begin with. Parliamentary government—and, *a fortiori*, democratic parliamentary government—is practicable only in a community whose members have a number of things in common—common political principles deriving from a common outlook that derives, in turn, from a common way of life. The different races, nations, civilizations, and religions of the present-day world are still far indeed from having even approached this degree of homogeneity and solidarity. They have been suddenly brought within point-blank range of each other through 'the annihilation of distance' by modern Western technology; and this terrific force that has brought them to-

gether without previous political or psychological pre-
paration has at the same time presented them with an
ultimatum: 'You must establish a world-government at
once. The penalty for failure, or even for delay, will be
self-annihilation.' Since we do not mean to put an end to
ourselves, we have to do what the ultimatum tells us.
We have to start building a world-state now on the best
design that is practicable at the moment. We cannot
afford to wait till we can be sure of being able to build
democracy into the world-state's original constitution.

To present-day Western ears the word 'world-state'
may sound visionary or chimaerical. For the last few
hundred years the Western peoples have been living
cooped up inside one or other of the local national states
that litter the present political map, and this modern
political experience of the West's makes it difficult for
modern Westerners to imagine living under any other
political dispensation. This Western experience is not,
however, typical. A larger part of the human race has
actually been living in a world-state during the larger
part of the time that has passed so far since the dawn of
civilization. To present-day Chinese minds, for instance,
it is national states, not a world-state, that will be un-
familiar. Every Chinese now alive who is of my age has
been born and brought up in a world-state that had been
in existence, off and on, for more than twenty-one
centuries before it was snuffed out at last in A.D. 1911.
I myself should have been born and brought up in
a world-state if I had been born in Britain, not in
A.D. 1889, as I was, but just fifteen hundred years
earlier.

The Roman Empire and the Chinese Empire were not, of course, world-states in the literal geographical sense of embracing the whole habitable and traversable surface of the planet. Actually they co-existed on its surface for several centuries without colliding with each other, and indeed without being more than dimly aware of each other's existence. A future world-state would, by contrast, have to be literally world-wide now that modern Western technology has knit up the whole surface of the planet into one single military arena. This geographical point is, however, a superficial one. On the political and psychological planes the Roman Empire and the Chinese Empire were authentic world-states. They were authentic because they solved the human problems that make a world-state difficult to build and at the same time indispensable to have. These historic world-states imposed peace on local communities that had been perpetually going to war with each other before they had been deprived of their sovereignty and independence. In the second place, these world-states by which the former local states had been subordinated and united succeeded eventually in winning for themselves the loyalty of the liquidated local states' former subjects. They succeeded in inspiring a common veneration and affection in the hearts of populations that differed from each other in race, language, culture, and religion. These two achievements in the sphere of human relations are all that we have to ask of a future world-state that would be literally world-wide. It is reassuring to recall that the political unity and the psychological solidarity that are, for us now, the alternatives to self-destruction have been

achieved in the past on at least two occasions. Both the
Chinese and the Roman world-state were successful in
giving peace and order to millions of human beings for
hundreds of years on end.

These historic achievements are so pertinent to our
own needs that it is worth inquiring how they were
brought about. One of the factors was a consideration
that is working in our minds, too, today. The Roman and
the Chinese world-state were each of them the only alternative to self-destruction; and in those two cases, as in
ours, human spirits were impelled to embark on an
enormously difficult political enterprise by the force of
their recoil from an awful penalty. They realized that
this penalty was in store for them if they were to flinch
from trying to establish a world-state or were to fail in
their attempt. But history also tells us that the direness
of the need might not have been enough, by itself, to
produce the achievement. The Roman and the Chinese
Empire each owed its establishment to the combined
action of two forces, a dire need and a statesman who
was equal to the occasion. These two historic saviours of
society were Augustus and Liu P'ang. Of the two,
Augustus is, of course, by far the better known in the
West, but that is only because the West is still parochial-
minded. Augustus's achievement, great though it was,
was not so great as Liu P'ang's. Augustus's world-state
lasted for less than seven centuries, even in its Levantine
core, and for less than five centuries in its western fringes.
Liu P'ang's world-state lasted for twenty-one centuries.
Both men's characters and careers are relevant to our
subject. The two were remarkably like each other, and

this is significant for us. It gives us a pointer towards identifying the kind of stateman that we need for serving as a saviour for our literally world-wide society.

Some of Liu P'ang's and Augustus's common characteristics are unattractive. Both men were unscrupulous and ruthless while they were thrusting their way up towards the summit. These early sins were forgiven them in retrospect in gratitude for the constructive and, on the whole, beneficent use that they made of the supreme power when once they had succeeded in concentrating this in their own hands. Both men were wily; and, whether or not we judge their early ruthlessness to have been indispensable for achieving their first objective of seizing power, we must concede that they needed to be wily not only in this first chapter of their careers but also in the second chapter, when they were using their achieved power to establish peace and order. Both men were almost infinitely patient and persistent; and this, at least, was a virtue that was not ambivalent. It shines out by contrast with the impatience and over-bearingness that had brought to naught the work of their respective forerunners, Ch'in Shih Hwang-ti and Julius Caesar. It was also a positive virtue in them that, when once they were in the saddle, they took pains to keep down their use of force to a minimum, to employ the least drastic possible means for attaining necessary objectives, and to save faces by ingenious legal fictions and other artifices. In the event, both men made it possible for millions of their fellow human beings to lead a considerably less wretched life than the life that they would undoubtedly have led if Liu P'ang and Augustus had not made themselves supreme by fair means or foul. I do not see how, in our world in its present plight, we can do without the services of a Liu P'ang or Augustus. If and when a modern counterpart of these previous saviours of society appears above our horizon, we shall, I believe, feel thankful for his arrival and shall be willing to take him as we find him. We must hope against hope to find him unstained by some, at any rate, of the crimes that Liu P'ang and Augustus both committed in the course of their hazardous ascents.

If we are on the look-out for an Augustus or Liu P'ang, in what direction are we to turn our eyes today? In the present-day world the two posts that confer on their occupants, at least ostensibly, the biggest concentration of personal power are the Presidency of the United States and the Chairmanship of the Praesidium of the Soviet Union. But it seems unlikely that either of these positions would prove to be a promising jumping-off ground for an attempt to acquire supreme power in the World as a whole. Any such attempt made from either of these points of vantage would infallibly be neutralized by countervailing resistance from the opposing point. In a world in which economics count for so much, it is conceivable that the road to supreme power might be an economic and not a political one. A wily organizer who had his fingers on one or other of the World's present key sources of material power might use this as his lever. He would be more likely, perhaps, to be an international public servant than a private business executive. He might be a banker (banking carried Lorenzo de' Medici to the summit in Florence). Alternatively our modern saviour of society might be one whose power was spiritual. A saviour of this kind is ardently to be hoped for; and there are grounds for such hope in the recent career of a great soul who, in retrospect, will perhaps be seen to tower above all his contemporaries. Long before the Mahatma Gandhi's life was cut short, he had become the saviour of India (and of Britain too, by building her a golden bridge for withdrawing from an invidious and untenable position). If Gandhi had lived longer, he might have done for the whole World something of what he had already done for about one-seventh of the World's inhabitants. The Mahatma Gandhi might still play this rôle posthumously. This would not be the first time that a violent death, suffered in a noble cause, had made a spiritual power posthumously irresistible. Moreover, Gandhi's principle of non-violence, and his technique for achieving mighty political results by non-violent means, answer precisely to mankind's needs in the Atomic Age. Gandhi launched his campaign for non-violent non-cooperation long before the atomic weapon had been dreamed of; and he might be credited with an inspired prescience if the reunciation of violence had not been an age-old Hindu spiritual ideal.

Gandhi's spirit will continue to work in the World, whether or not Gandhi has an avatar to bring his mission to fulfilment on a world-wide scale. If he does have an avatar, this avatar is perhaps more likely to make its appearance in a Hindu or Buddhist sage or saint than in an adherent of any of the religions of the South-West-Asian group. A Sunni Muslim candidate for the rôle would draw on himself the opposition of Shi 'ites, Christians, and Jews; a Roman Catholic Christian candidate would draw on himself the opposition of Protestant and Orthodox Christians, as well as Jews and Muslims. A representative of Hinduism or Buddhism would perhaps be less likely to produce this provocative effect on the adherents of other religions. He would be less likely in so far as his own attitude towards other religions might be less censorious or militant. This last proviso applies, of course, to any of the possible candidates.

I think this is as far as, or possibly farther than, it is profitable to go in trying to peer into the future. We are here in the realm of conjecture. Yet our experience of the past does at least throw a flickering gleam of light on the darkness ahead.

AMERICA AND
THE WORLD REVOLUTION

I

THE SHOT HEARD ROUND
THE WORLD

I DO not need to justify my subject: 'America and the World Revolution.' There can be few contemporary questions that are of such outstanding importance and interest as this one is. Its obvious significance was what tempted me to offer it—and now, having confessed that I *offered* the subject, I do feel moved to apologize, not for the subject itself, but for the lecturer. The subject is not only important and interesting; it is also delicate and hazardous to at least an equal degree. Even an American speaker might quail at the prospect of addressing this audience on this subject, though for him this would be a family affair; he would be talking to his own countrymen and countrywomen. And now here am I, a foreigner, having the audacity to stand up and talk to you on this formidable theme. I have not even been drafted to do this; I am a brash volunteer; so the consequences, whatever they may be, are entirely on my own head.

I am not going to try to avoid awkward consequences by setting out to be tactful and diplomatic. There would be no point in speaking on this subject at all if one did not express one's opinion frankly. And it is a subject on which almost any opinions are likely to be controversial; the way one puts one's opinions may, unavoidably, be

77

provocative; in fact, one is risking getting oneself into hot
water. Well, there is one point in my favour that I can
plead with complete sincerity. In so far as I make criticisms of America and Americans, I shall be conscious,
in almost every case, that these criticisms also apply to
my own country and own countrymen. I shall not be
able to say to myself: 'There, but for the grace of God,
go Britain and the British.' The British have, I should
say, already made all those mistakes that the Americans
are now making, or may now be in danger of making.
Britain's position in the World in the nineteenth century had, after all, a good deal in common with
America's position in the World today. The load on
British shoulders then was not, I suppose, as heavy as
the present load on American shoulders. Your present
position is a bit more lonely and a good deal more responsible than ours has ever been. Still, we have had a
foretaste of your present experience; and it has been a
close enough foretaste to throw a present-day Englishman into a fit of fear and trembling when his subject is
America's response to the challenge that has now been
presented to America in her turn.

Every criticism that I shall venture to make of present-
day America could, as I have said, probably be made of
pre-1914 Britain to the same effect. I shall often be drawing the parallel. If I skip this exercise in some cases, this
will be for the good reason that the present and the
future are of greater concern to us than the past is.
Britain's ascendency in the World is now past history;
America's is present politics, and the question how
America is going to acquit herself in her present ordeal

is a question of life and death, not just for America herself, but for the whole human race. Therefore America's
affairs are now no longer just private affairs of her
own; *ex officio* they are public affairs in which the
whole World is genuinely and therefore legimately
concerned. The World's concern is legitimate, because the World's future is at stake in America's
action.

This is annoying for America; it is more than just
annoying; it is excruciating. Privacy is one of the necessities of human life, and to lose one's privacy makes life
difficult to bear. This is the reason why people who have
had the misfortune to be born royal sometimes make
frantic efforts to break their way out into private life.
To be born royal means being condemned in advance
to live one's life in public, and this is an almost intolerable servitude. One may incur this servitude through the
accident of birth, or one may incur it through force of
circumstances. America has incurred her present servitude in the second of these ways, and this makes it all
the more irksome. If one has been born a slave, one may
become more or less conditioned to slavery before one
has become conscious of the painfulness of one's position. If one is enslaved later on in life, it is more difficult
to become reconciled to this cruel change for the worse
in one's circumstances.

Power and wealth have advantages that are obvious;
but there are also automatic penalties attached to them,
and these are severe. The strong and the rich are not
only held to account up to the limits of their actual
responsibility. They are also made the scapegoats for

anything that goes wrong anywhere, even when it is not their fault and even when it would have been beyond their power to make things go better. Worse than that, if the strong and rich use their power and wealth generously for other people's benefit, they will be accused of having done so for interested motives, and they will be repaid with ingratitude. I speak with feeling about this, because I am just old enough to remember the time when Britain was still rich and strong enough to be the principal target for poorer and weaker people's malice. Baiting is one of mankind's oldest games, but the victim has to be a substantial one if the game is to be fun. Twisting the lion's tail ceases to be rewarding if the lion shrinks to the size of a cat; but if a buzzard swells to the size of an eagle, it then becomes worthwhile to pull out the bird's tail-feathers. It is not easy to adjust oneself to a rapid decrease in one's wealth and power, but the transition is eased by one consoling form of relief. In being relieved of power and wealth, one is automatically relieved from odium. *Experto crede*. I am speaking from my own country's experience in my own lifetime. We have been released from the odium that used to hang round Britain's neck like the Ancient Mariner's murdered albatross. The neck that is now adorned by the corpse of that albatross is America's. When we British look at America nowadays, our feelings are mixed. We feel consoled for the recent change in our position in the World; at the same time we sympathize with you for the change in your position. I do hope that the second of these two feelings will make itself obvious to you in this present course of lectures by a British speaker. In examining America's situation in the World today, I can say, with my hand on my heart, that my feelings are sympathetic, not malicious. After all, mere regard for self-interest, apart from any more estimable considerations, would deter America's allies from wishing America ill. If, *absit omen*, America were to be worsted by her present ordeal, this would be as great a misfortune for her friends and associates as it would be for America herself.

I suppose many of us in this room have stood, more than once in our lives, on the bridge at Concord, Massachusetts, and have then crossed the bridge to read, engraved on a bronze plaque, a poem that we already knew by heart. As far as I remember, I first got to know this poem of Emerson's through being given it, at school, to translate into Greek verse. The school was in England, not in America. The date must have been about 1905. That would be one hundred and thirty years after the day on which the historic shot had been fired by embattled American farmers. That was time enough to have made it possible for English schoolmasters and English schoolboys to look back at what had happened in April 1775 without having our vision blurred by irrelevant national sore feelings. What thrilled us, in England in 1905, at the sound of that shot was the point that has been put inimitably by Emerson in the eight monosyllabic words of his immortal line. We forgot that the shot had been aimed at red-coats. We remembered that it had been heard round the World. That shot now meant for us, too, what it had meant for your ancestors. I myself, for instance, made my pilgrimage to the bridge at Concord the first time I visited the United States, which was in 1925.

A poet knows how to sum up in one line what it takes an historian at least several pages to recite. Within these last one hundred and eighty-six years the sound of that American shot has been travelling round and round the globe like a Russian sputnik. It had been heard in France before the eighteenth century was over. It was heard in Spanish America and in Greece while the nineteenth century was still young. In 1848, when the nineteenth century was not yet quite half spent, the sound reverberated, like a thunderclap, over the whole of Continental Europe. It was heard in Italy, and Italy arose from the dead. The Italian Risorgimento was evoked by that American shot. The sound was heard in Paris again in 1871; this time the Commune was Paris's response to it. Travelling on eastward, the sound touched off the Russian revolution of 1905, the Persian revolution of 1906, and the Turkish revolution of 1908. By that date it had already roused the Founding Fathers of the Indian National Congress. I believe, by the way, that the original instigator of the Indian Congress Movement was an Englishman. If I am right about this, that Englishman launched a far bigger movement than he can have realized at the time. The Indian Congress Movement has been the mother of all the independence movements in all the Asian and African countries that, till recently, have been under the rule of West European colonial powers. But, anyway, whoever may deserve the credit for having started the Indian Congress Movement, the inspiration of it came from the sound of that

American shot as this sound travelled over the Indian sub-continent on its eastward course. By this time it had gathered a speed that must have been greater than the speed of light. By 1911, the year in which the sound was heard in China, it had already been heard on the far side of the pacific, in Mexico. It had already touched off the Mexican Revolution of 1910.

By 1910, the eastward-travelling American sputnik had come round, full circle, to re-visit the New World. But it did not stop at that point. Its momentum was still unexhausted. It sped forward for the second time over the Atlantic to re-awaken the Old World's seven sleepers with still more thunderous reverberations than it had detonated at its first visitation. In 1917 Russia heard that American sound for the second time, and this time she heard it with a vengeance. Turkey heard it for the second time after the end of the First World War, and this time the sound touched off the radical Westernizing Turkish revolution led by Mustafa Kemal Atatürk. Compared with this second Turkish revolution of 1919-28, the Turkish revolution of 1908 had been half-hearted. In April 1923, just one hundred and forty-eight years after the firing of that shot, far away, at the bridge at Concord, Massachusetts, I heard the sound reach Ankara, Turkey's new capital, where I happened, at that moment, to find myself. There and then, I was given an inkling of what it must have felt like to be in the streets of Paris in 1789 or beside the bridge at Concord in 1775.

The sound did not flag or falter. It went on making its second circuit of the globe. In China, in 1948, its second visitation produced the same enormously enhanced effects as its previous second visitations in Russia and in Turkey. Speeding across the Pacific for the second time, the indefatigable sound called the Bolivian miners to arms and roused the Guatemalan peasants to demand a re-distribution of the land. In 1960 it roused the peasants of Cuba. Fidel Castro must have been surprised and gratified by the attention that he has won for himself in the United States. He has had the advantage of standing so close to the American people's ear that, by shouting into it, he has been able to make it tingle. He wanted to annoy America, and he succeeded. But, if he had not had the luck to be so close to you, his oratory would have been drowned; for, before the end of 1960, the sound of the embattled American farmers' shot had crossed the Atlantic for the third time and had roused up the whole of Africa from Sharpville to Algiers.

At this moment at which I am speaking to you here in this room, I am surprised that I have succeeded, like Fidel Castro, in making my annoying words heard above that other sound's roar. For, by now, the sound of the embattled farmers' shot 'is gone out through all the Earth', to quote the Psalmist's words. The noise has become world-wide and it has become deafening. Jefferson hit the mark when he said that 'the disease of liberty is catching'.

What we are hearing now, above the echoing sound of that American shot, is the answering voice of the mass of mankind. This two-thirds—or is it three-quarters?—of the World's population is still living only just above the starvation line and is still frequently falling below even that wretched line into death-dealing famine. Since the time when our pre-human ancestors became human, this majority of the human race has never dreamed, before today, that there would ever be any change for the better in its hard lot. Since the dawn of civilization, about 5000 years ago, the World's peasantry has carried the load of civilization on its back without receiving any appreciable share in civilization's benefits. These benefits have been monopolized by a tiny privileged minority, and, until yesterday, this injustice was inevitable. Till the modern industrial revolution began to get up steam, technology was not capable of producing more than a tiny surplus after meeting the requirements of bare subsistence. In our time, technology is coming within sight of being able to produce enough of civilization's material benefits to provide for the whole human race. If technology does make it possible to get rid of the odious ancient difference in fortune between the few rich and the innumerable poor, future generations will perhaps bless the Industrial Revolution in retrospect, and will think kindly of its British, American and German pioneers.

We already have the means for making a start in improving the lot of the great depressed majority of our fellow human beings. But, in the last resort, we human beings have to do things for ourselves. The World's peasantry cannot hope to improve its lot substantially unless it can awake from its age-old lethargy. It is being awakened at this moment by the sound of that American shot as that sound circles the globe for the third time. That sound has now been heard by the World's whole depressed majority, and we, the affluent minority, are now hearing the majority's reply. At last, the majority is shaking off the fatalism that has been para- lysing it since the beginning of time. It is becoming alive to the truth that an improvement in its lot is now pos- sible. More than that, it is realizing that it can do some- thing towards this by its own efforts. Go to India; visit some of the thousands of villages there in which the Community Development Plan is already in operation; and you will see, with your own eyes, this new hope and purposefulness and energy breaking into flower. This is, to my mind, the most wonderful sight that there is to be seen in the present-day world. And this world-revolu- tion of the peasantry is the most glorious revolution that there has been in the World's history so far.

Well, perhaps I ought to have said 'the most glorious *secular* revolution'; for the religious revolutions may have been more glorious; and these may also, in the long run, prove to have had still greater and more bene- ficent effects. By the religious revolutions I mean the advent of the World's missionary religions: Buddhism, Christianity, Islam, and the others. The new world revolution of the peasantry perhaps cannot properly be called a religious revolution. At the same time it is un- questionably a spiritual one. It is true that the objectives that are its first aim are of a material kind. These ma- terial objectives are as elementary as they are indis- pensable for making a start. They are such fundamental things as a concrete lining and lip for the village well, to protect the water from being contaminated; a concrete surface for the village lanes, to redeem them from being wallows of pestilent filth; a dirt-road to link the village up with the nearest main road; and, after that, a village school. When a village reaches the stage of building a school and finding the means to provide a living for a schoolmaster, it is already beginning to raise a spiritual mansion on the preliminary material foundations. Without the foundations, the building could not go up. But the material foundations are a means to a spiritual end. And what could be more obviously spiritual than the awakening of hope and purposefulness and energy that is the driving force behind the whole of this glorious revolution? This driving force is the last and greatest of the revolutionary forces that have been released, all round the World, by the sound of a shot that was fired, on an April day, by embattled American farmers.

This exhilarating sound has not only roused the peoples of the World to action in their own homelands; it has also drawn them, like a magnet, to the land in which the shot was fired and from which the sound has gone forth. For a century, European farmers flocked to the United States in order to become American farmers, and, as the Industrial Revolution got up steam on both sides of the Atlantic, European industrial workers were soon crossing the Atlantic westward in the farmers' wake. The tide of immigration into the United States began to flow mightily within a few years of the end of the Napoleonic Wars. It went on flowing till the outbreak of the First World War in 1914. And, as it flowed, it gathered volume. Before it was abruptly checked in 1914 by the action of the belligerent European governments that were concerned to conserve their cannon-fodder, the annual total of immigrants had risen to about two million in more than one year after the turn of the century.

When I think of this century of massive immigration from Europe into Europe's American promised land, my mind focuses on my memory's picture of an old farmer, Bavarian-born, whom I met on my first visit to this country, now nearly thirty-six years ago. His farm was in East Central Kentucky, where I was staying with a college friend of mine. At home in Bavaria, this farmer had had no farm of his own and no prospect of ever acquiring one there. It had been the hope of winning one in the New World that had lured him across the Atlantic. Though he had emigrated while he was still a young man, he had not arrived till some year in the eighteen-nineties, and by that time, of course, all the best land in the state had been taken up long ago. In Kentucky by the eighteen-nineties, settlement had been going on for more than a hundred years. All the same, this Bavarian farmer had come in time still to be a pioneer. In the western foothills of the Appalachians—'the Knobs' is their local name—he had hit upon a valley that was still unreclaimed because no predecessor of his had found it sufficiently inviting. The Bavarian had seized on that valley and had made it fruitful. To transform it had been his life-work. He had not only made it yield him enough for raising a family. By the time his sons were grown up—and there were several of them—the father had also saved enough to be able to buy for each son a better farm than the father's own. But the old man would never buy a better farm for himself. The valley-farm had been his life-work, and, more than that, it had been his European dream translated into an American reality. As a boy in Bavaria he had dreamed of one day having a farm of his own if he could screw up his courage to pull up his roots and cross the Ocean. In this unpromising valley in Kentucky he had made his farm and his farm had made him. Nothing this side of death would part him from it.

Multiply this Bavarian-American farmer by some millions and you have a revolution inside America to match those revolutions all round the World of which I have given you a breathless catalogue. America's revolution on her own ground and her revolutions abroad have been like each other in everything that is important in them. They have both been set going by the shot fired in April 1775; they have both been triumphs over social injustice, poverty, and hopelessness. These revolutions are true daughters of the American Revolution, and to have fathered this mighty brood is indeed an achievement to be proud of. And now come the paradox, and, I should also say, the tragedy. At the moment when the sound of that historic American shot was circling this planet for the third time, at the moment when the American revolutionary spirit had come within sight of inspiring the whole human race, America herself disowned paternity, at least for the younger and less decorous batches of her offspring.

It has been suggested recently by at least one American student of American history that America did not wait till the twentieth century to dissociate herself from the World's response to the resounding American shot's reverberations. The founding fathers of the United

States lived to witness the French Revolution, and at least one of the most eminent of them, John Adams, put on record his repudiation and rejection of the American Revolution's French eldest daughter after she had jilted Lafayette and had plunged into Jacobinism. I owe my knowledge of the following passage to an article by William Henry Chamberlin in *The Wall Street Journal* of 31 March 1961. John Adams is quoted by Mr Chamberlain as having said that 'Helvetius and Rousseau preached to the French nation liberty till they made them the most mechanical slaves; equality, till they destroyed all equity; humanity, until they became weasels and African panthers; and fraternity, till they cut one another's throats like Roman gladiators'.

This bitter verdict on the Jacobin revolution gives us some notion of how John Adams and like-minded American contemporaries of his would have reacted to the Communist revolution, if they could have lived to witness this still more violent subsequent response to the echoes of the revolution which the founding fathers themselves had launched. The founding fathers had, no doubt, carried their own revolution just as far as they had intended, and evidently some of them were unwilling to see revolution, either at home or abroad, go even one inch farther. This is indicated by the bitterness of those words of John Adams's that I have just quoted. But his words are not only bitter; they are also ironic. They bring out the irony of the contrast between intentions and results; and this is one of the perennial ironies of human life. It is seldom indeed that the consequences of human action work out according to plan; and one might venture on the generalization that they never work out as intended when the action is of the violent kind represented by revolution and war. The more violent the initial act, the more likely it will be that its consequences will escape control. Has there ever been a revolution or a war that has produced the results, and none other than the results, that its authors intended and expected? The American revolutionaries, like their French counterparts, and unlike at least one celebrated batch of Roman gladiators, were not 'too proud to fight'; and they could not fire their shot without its being heard by other ears, and without its being taken as a signal for non-American, and perhaps un-American, action. In illustrating the vanity of human wishes by the example of the Jacobins, John Adams was unconsciously passing judgement on himself as well. *Fabula de te narratur* is the comment that he invites in retrospect. But Adams's anti-Jacobin invective, which thus recoils like a boomerang on Adams himself, leaves his co-founding father Jefferson unscathed. Jefferson recognized that the price of political liberty would be 'turbulence', and he was not distressed by this prospect. 'I hold,' he wrote to Madison, 'that a little rebellion now and then is a good thing, and as necessary in the political world as storing in the physical.'

Thus Adams's conservatism was not shared by all the founding fathers; and Emerson was not the first American to acclaim the World Revolution and to recognize it as being the American Revolution's offspring. America had already given a blessing to the late eighteenth-century and early nineteenth-century revolutions in

Europe which it would be difficult for her ever to revoke, since it has been written into the map of American place-names. The names of the Corsican, Greek, Polish, and Hungarian revolutionary leaders Paoli, Ypsilandi, Kosciusko, and Kossuth have been thus immortalized. On the other hand, no Leninburg or Trotskyville has ever jumped out of the map of the United States to catch my eye. Of course there is less room for putting new names on this map nowadays than there used to be. Yet, if tomorrow a new territory of the United States were to be staked out on the face of the Moon, I do not think that any of the mushroom cities there would be likely to be called Fidel, though Fidel is really rather a beautiful name if American lips could pronounce it dispassionately.

Today America is no longer the inspirer and leader of the World Revolution, and I have an impression that she is embarrassed and annoyed when she is reminded that this was her original mission. No one else laid this mission upon America. She chose it for herself, and for one hundred and forty-two years, reckoning from the year 1775, she pursued this revolutionary mission with an enthusiasm which has proved deservedly infectious. By contrast, America is today the leader of a world-wide anti-revolutionary movement in defence of vested interests. She now stands for what Rome stood for. Rome consistently supported the rich against the poor in all foreign communities that fell under her sway; and, since the poor, so far, have always and everywhere been far more numerous than the rich, Rome's policy made for inequality, for injustice, and for the least happiness of the greatest number. America's decision to adopt Rome's role has been deliberate, if I have gauged it right. It has been deliberate, yet, in the spirit that animates this recent American movement in reverse, I miss the enthusiasm and the confidence that made the old revolutionary America irresistible. Lafayette pays a high psychological price when he transforms himself into Metternich. Playing Metternich is not a happy role. It is not a hero's role, and not a winner's, and the player knows it. But, in those early nineteenth-century years when the real Metternich was fighting his losing battle to shore up the rickety edifice of restored 'legitimacy', who in the World would have guessed that America, of all countries, would one day cast herself for Metternich's dreary part?

What has happened? The simplest account of it is, I suppose, that America has joined the minority. In 1775 she was in the ranks of the majority, and this is one reason why the American Revolution has evoked a world-wide response. For the non-American majority of the majority, the American revolutionary appeal has been as attractive as it was for eighteenth-century America herself. Eighteenth-century America was still appreciably poorer than the richest of the eighteenth-century West European countries: Britain, Holland, the Austrian Netherlands, France. No doubt America was, even then, already considerably richer than Asia or Africa; yet, even measured by this standard, her wealth at that time was not enormous. What has happened? While the sound of the shot fired beside the bridge at Concord has been three times circling the globe, and has each time been inciting all people outside America, to redouble their revolutionary efforts, America herself has been engaged on another job than the one that she finished on her own soil in 1783. She has been winning the West and has been mastering the technique of industrial productivity. In consequence, she has become rich beyond all precedent. And, when the American sputnik's third round raised the temperature of the World Revolution to a height that was also unprecedented, America felt herself impelled to defend the wealth that she had now gained against the mounting revolutionary forces that she herself had first called into existence.

What was the date at which America boxed the compass in steering her political course? As I see it, this date is pin-pointed by three events: the reaction in the United States to the second Russian revolution of 1917 and the two United States immigration restriction acts of 1921 and 1924.

The American reaction to the Bolshevik revolution in Russia was not, of course, peculiar to the American people. It was the same as the reaction of the rich people in all countries. Only, in the United States, it was a nation-wide reaction, because, in the United States, the well-to-do section of the population had become, by that time, a large majority, not the small minority that the rich have been and still are in most other parts of the World so far.

Rich people, not only in the United States but everywhere, have, I think, taken Communism in a very personal way. They have seen in Communism a threat to their pocket-books. So Communism, even when it has raised its head in some far-away country, has not felt to the rich like a foreign affair; the threat has seemed close and immediate, like the threat from gangsters in the streets of one's home town. I think this explains the fact—and I am sure this is the fact—that Russian Communist aggression has got under the skins of the well-to-do in the Western World, while German nationalist aggression has not angered them to the same degree. This relative complacency towards German aggressiveness, as contrasted with the violence of the reaction to Russian aggressiveness, has made an impression on me because, I confess, it makes me bristle. I have noticed it among the rich minority in my own country, and I have noticed it still more among a wider circle of people in the United States. It is a rather startling piece of self-exposure. It is startling because, among the various dangers with which we have been threatened in our time, the danger to our personal property is not the one that we ought really to take most tragically. As a matter of fact, the well-to-do Western middle class would have been fleeced economically by the Germans, as thoroughly as this could be done by any Communists, if Germany had happened to win either the first or the second world war—and Germany came within an ace of winning each of these wars in turn. But the tragic loss that would have been inflicted on the Western World by a German victory would have been the loss of our political and our spiritual liberty. In two fearful wars that have been brought upon us by Germany within the span of a single life-time, we have saved our liberty at an immense loss in infinitely precious human lives. We have had no war with Russia in our life-time, and the Western and the

Communist camp are not doomed to go to war with each other, though at present the common threat of self-annihilation in an atomic third world war hangs over us all.

Of course someone might reply to what I have just been saying by admitting the whole of my indictment of Germany but pointing out, at the same time, that Russia, too, threatens our political and spiritual freedom, besides threatening just our pockets. This is true. Yet, if I had to make the terrible choice between being conquered by a nationalist Germany and being conquered by a Communist Russia, I myself would opt for Russian Communism as against German nationalism. I would opt for it as being the less odious of the two régimes to live under. Nationalism, German or other, has no aim beyond the narrow-hearted aim of pursuing one's own national self-interest at the expense of the rest of the human race. By contrast, Communism has in it an element of universalism. It does stand in principle for winning social justice for that great majority of mankind that has hitherto received less than its fair share of the benefits of civilization. I know very well that, in politics, principle is never more than partially translated into practice; I know that the generous-minded vein in Communism is marred by the violent and intolerant-minded vein in it. I also recognize that Communism in both Russia and China has been partly harnessed to a Russian and a Chinese nationalism that is no more estimable than German nationalism or any other nationalism is. Yet, when all this has been said, I still find myself feeling that the reaction of rich individuals and rich nations in

the West to Communism since 1917 has been an 'acid
test', to use President Wilson's memorable words. Anyway, it is, I think, indisputable that the reaction in the
United States to Communism in and since the year 1917
has been a symptom of a reversal of America's political
course. It is a sign, I think, that the American people is
now feeling and acting as a champion of an affluent
minority's vested interests, in dramatic contrast to
America's historic role as the revolutionary leader of the
depressed majority of mankind.

The United States immigration restriction acts of 1921
and 1924 are, I believe, pointers to the same change in the
American people's attitude during and immediately after
the First World War. Naturally I realize the urgent
practical considerations that moved the Administration
and the Congress to enact this legislation. The First
World War had just brought to light a disturbing
feature in this country's domestic life: I mean, the
persistence of the hyphen. An appreciable number of
United States citizens, and of immigrants who were on
their way to becoming citizens, had proved still to have
divided loyalties. The American melting-pot had not yet
purged out of their hearts the last residue of their hereditary attachment to their countries of origin on the European side of the Atlantic. There was evidently a long
road still to travel before the process of assimilation
would be completed, and this race between assimilation
and immigration might never be won for Americanism
unless the annual intake of immigrants were drastically
reduced. Moreover, the pre-war immigrants were under
criticism not only for still being pulled two ways by

divided loyalties; they were also under suspicion of perhaps not being representative samples of the best European human material. The introduction of an annual quota would enable the United States Bureau of Immigration to sift the candidates for admission and to select those who promised to make the best future American citizens, and the policy of restriction was thus recommended by a eugenic motive as well as by a political one.

These considerations, by themselves, would have made some measure of restriction and selection desirable after the First World War anyway. But the main motive for the enactment of the acts of 1921 and 1924 was, I believe, a different one. Europe had just been ravaged by a war of unprecedented magnitude and severity. European belligerent governments had stopped their subjects from emigrating in order to conserve their supplies of cannon-fodder. And, now that the war was over, it was feared in the United States that the flow of immigration would start again, and this time in an unprecedented volume. A flood of penniless Europeans might pour into the United States in quest of fortunes in the New World to compensate for ruin in the Old World, and this probable rush of millions of European paupers to win a share in America's prosperity was felt to be a menace to the economic interests of the existing inhabitants of the United States, who had a monopoly of America's wealth at present.

If I am right in this diagnosis of the main motive for the United States immigration restriction acts of 1921 and 1924, the American people went on the defensive at this time against the impact of European immigration for the same reason that made America react so strongly against Communism. Both these reactions were those of a rich man who is concerned to defend his private property against the importunity of a mass of pooerer people who are surging all round him and are loudly demanding a share in the rich man's wealth.

What would have been the effects on America's economic life if immigration into the United States had been left, down to this day, as free as it was during the century ending in 1921? Presumably the present population of the United States would have been much larger than it actually is, but it does not necessarily follow that the average income per head would have been lower. Experience tells us that a country's total annual product is not a fixed amount. It may be increased by various factors. One of these stimuli to production may be a steep rise in the volume of population through a reinforcement of the natural increase by immigration. For example, the massive and unrestricted immigration into West Germany from East Germany since the end of the Second World War has been one, at least, of the causes of West Germany's unexpected and surprising post-war economic prosperity. On this analogy it is conceivable that the economic effects of the United States immigration restriction acts of 1921 and 1924 was contrary to the legislators' intentions and expectations. While conserving the previous income per head of the existing population of the United States, the immigration restriction acts may have prevented the income per head from rising so fast and so high as it might have done if immigration had been left unrestricted. A continuance of unrestricted immigration might also perhaps have saved the United States from the great depression of the nineteen-thirties. These are hypothetical questions which even an economist might find it hard to answer, and I am not an economist. But I would suggest to you that, whatever the economic consequences of those immigration restriction acts may have been, these economic consequences have not been the most important. The political and psychological consequences have, I should say, counted for more, and these non-economic consequences have, I should also say, been unfortunate for America as well as for Europe.

So long as immigration into the United States from Europe was unrestricted, America's ever open door kept America in touch with the common lot of the human race. The human race, as a whole, was poor, as it still is; and America was then still a poor man's country. She was a poor man's country in the stimulating sense of being the country that was the poor man's hope. She was the country, of all countries, in which a poor immigrant could look forward to improving his economic position by his own efforts. America did not, of course, even then, offer this opportunity to immigrants from the whole of the Old World. The opportunity was always restricted to immigrants from one small corner of the Old World, namely Europe. All the same, so long as America still offered herself as even just the European poor man's hope, she retained her footing as part of the majority of the human race. In so far as she has closed her doors since 1921, she has cut herself off from the majority. This self-insulation is the inevitable penalty of finding that one has become rich and then taking steps to protect one's new-found well-being. The impulse to protect wealth, if one has it, is one of the natural human impulses. It is not particularly sinful, but it automatically brings a penalty with it that is out of proportion to its sinfulness. This penalty is isolation. It is a fearful thing to be isolated from the majority of one's fellow-creatures, and this will continue to be the social and moral price of wealth so long as poverty continues to be the normal condition of the World's ordinary men and women.

I will close this first lecture in the present series by trying to drive this point home in a piece of fantasy. Let us imagine a transmigration of souls in reverse. Let us slip our own generation's souls into the bodies of the generation of 1775, and then set the reel of history unwinding with this change in its make-up. The result that we shall obtain by this sleight of hand will be startlingly different from the actual course of events in 1775 and thereafter. The Declaration of Independence will now be made, not in Philadelphia, but at Westminster. King George III will raise his standard, not at the Court of St. James's, but at Independence Hall (of course that building will not bear its historic revolutionary name; it will be called 'Royal Hall' or 'Legitimacy Hall' or some other respectable conservative name of the kind). The other George, George Washington, will take command of his royal namesake's army. There will be no Continental Congress here in Philadelphia for George Washington to serve. The revolutionary parliament will be on the other side of the Ocean. It will be at Westminster. And the revolutionary leader will not be a

George, but a Charles, namely Charles James Fox. The bridge beside which the embattled farmers will fire their shot will not be the bridge at Concord. The flood that it spans will be the Thames. The shot will be heard round the World, but it will be an Old-World shot, not a New-World one.

This nonsense that I have just been talking will have had its use if it has illustrated my thesis. I am maintaining that, since 1917, America has reversed her role in the World. She has become the arch-conservative power instead of the arch-revolutionary one. Stranger still, she has made a present of her glorious discarded role to the country which was the arch-conservative power in the nineteenth century, the country which, since 1946, has been regarded by America as being America's Enemy Number One. America has presented her historic revolutionary role to Russia.

Is this reversal of roles America's irrevocable choice? Is it a choice that she can afford to make? And, if she were to change her mind once again, would it now still be possible for America to rejoin her own revolution after having parted company with it forty-four years ago? I shall be taking up these questions in the second and third lectures in this series.

THE HANDICAP OF AFFLUENCE

SINCE the time when pre-Man became human, nearly all human beings have been poor. The poor man or poor community is normal; the rich is exceptional. The penalty of affluence is that it cuts one off from the common lot, common experience, and common fellowship. In a sense, it outlaws one automatically from one's human birthright of membership in the great human family. This fellowship of Man is one of the stations on the road whose terminus is the Kingdom of God and whose entrance-gate is the needle's eye. The innumerable host of the ants can slip through, but the camels cannot get by—not even one at a time, in single file.

This fundamental fact of human life has a bearing on a present-day political puzzle. This puzzling question is why America is at present being worsted, on the whole, in her competition with Russia for winning the friendship and support of the great non-American and non-Russian majority of the human race. There is, I am afraid, little doubt that this is the fact, and at first sight it seems hard to explain. It is puzzling for several reasons.

Everyone knows that America never wanted or sought the international position of leadership in which she now finds herself. When America says 'Nolo episcopari', everyone knows that her protestation is sincere, not hypocritical. As a matter of historical fact, America may have brought her present undesired leadership upon herself. I myself believe that she did condemn herself to this when, after the First World War, she refused to become a member of the League of Nations. America's relapse into isolation after the First World War made the Second World War inevitable. And the Second World War made it inevitable that America should be drawn into this war too and that, this time, she should find herself unable to withdraw again. Yet, if it is true that America has brought her present leadership on herself by her own acts, it is also manifest that her intention, in acting as she did, was to produce exactly the opposite result to what has actually happened. Her intention was to revert to her nineteenth-century position of aloofness and non-commitment. Her defeat of her own intentions by her own acts has been ironical, but it has not been America's peculiar fate. It is a common human experience to defeat one's own intentions by the very single-mindedness of one's efforts to carry these intentions out. The most ingenious and most cynical interpreter of recent American history would feel it far-fetched to suggest that America did what she did with the intention of bringing about what has in fact happened.

Everyone also knows that America today has no ambition to increase her territorial possessions. The islands in the Western Pacific that the United States kept in her hands after the Second World War were a small prize to have pocketed after a total victory in a war on a world-wide scale. The United States' latest previous territorial acquisitions were mostly not the fruits of military conquest. I am thinking of the Gadsden Purchase and Alaska and Hawaii and the Virgin Islands. Puerto Rico was conquered in the Spanish War, but, if I am right, this is the only one of America's conquests from Spain on that occasion that America has retained. It is true that, in the Mexican War, the United States did make conquests on a scale comparable to the scale of Russia's nineteenth-century conquests. But purchase, not conquest, has been the typical means by which the area of the United States has been increased. The Louisiana Purchase is the classical case. The United States' early ambition to acquire political sovereignty over Canada was renounced completely long ago. Thus, though the United States has, in fact, grown as vigorously as Topsy, her record, apart from the conquests made in the Mexican War, is on the whole a reassuring one for the rest of the World.

I have put in the *caveat* 'on the whole' because history tells us that conquest and annexation are not the only means, or indeed the most frequent and most effective means, by which empires have been built up in the past. The history of the Roman Empire's growth, for instance, is instructive when one is considering the present-day American Empire's structure and prospects. The principal method by which Rome established her political supremacy in her world was by taking her weaker neighbours under her wing and protecting them against her and their stronger neighbours. Rome's relation with these protégées of hers was a treaty relation. Juridically they retained their previous status of sovereign independence. The most that Rome asked of them in terms of territory was the cession, here and there, of a patch of ground for the plantation of a Roman fortress to provide for the common security of Rome's allies and Rome herself. There is little evidence that, in making the many political arrangements that she did make along these lines, Rome was harbouring ulterior designs which she did not avow. We can believe in Rome's sincerity almost as unreservedly as we do believe in America's. But in Rome's case the historian has the advantage of knowing the end of the story. We can believe in Rome's sincerity, but we cannot shut our eyes to the eventual results. As the centuries passed, the vast territories of Rome's one-time allies became just as much a part of the Roman Empire as the less extensive territories of Rome's one-time enemies which Rome had deliberately and overtly annexed.

Let me call your attention again to the Roman practice of establishing Roman bases, by agreement, on the territories of allied states. This Roman precedent is pertinent to our present inquiry because, in our time, this method of extending the range of a country's power has been adopted, on a considerable scale, by the United States in her turn. I am old enough to remember the impression made on me, when I was a school-boy, by an issue of the *Illustrated London News* in which there were pictures of scenes in the revolution by which Panamá detached itself from Colombia and set itself up as a sovereign independent republic. One of the sequels to this Latin American revolution was the perpetual lease of the Canal Zone by the new Republic of Panamá to the United States. This celebrated lease has, as we know, been one in a series. Cuba, for instance, leased the Guantánamo base to the United States in token of gratitude for her liberation from Spain thanks to American military intervention. Great Britain leased the bases in the British West Indies to the United States as a *quid pro quo* for the gift of the hundred destroyers in 1940. Since the Second World War, the number of America's allies has greatly increased, and the number of bases leased to the United States in their territories has increased, I should guess, at least proportionately.

When the short-lived West Indian Confederation attained independence, America made the gracious gesture of giving back to the Confederation some of the West Indian bases that it had leased from the United Kingdom at a time when what had now become the Confederation was still British colonial territory. I am reminded of a similar gracious gesture that was made by Rome to the Greeks after she had liberated Greece from the ascendancy of the Kingdom of Macedon. Rome then voluntarily evacuated three former Macedonian fortresses—the so-called 'fetters of Greece'—which Macedon had been compelled to cede to Rome as part of the penalty for her defeat. This Roman act of generosity was sincerely meant, and it was received by the Greeks with enthusiasm. All the same, I remember that this was not the end of the story of Rome's relations with Greece. Corinth, which was one of the three Greek fortresses that had been liberated and evacuated by the Romans in 196 B.C., was rased to the ground by the Romans just fifty years later.

America today does not want additional territory for

herself, but she does set great store today by the acquisition and retention of bases on allied territory. These are of vital importance to her now because it is her policy to try to prevent Russia, on her side, from acquiring additional territory either by outright annexation or by the subtler process of reducing allies to the status of satellites. For this negative purpose the United States wishes today to have as many bases as possible within as close a range as possible of the Soviet Union, and this American strategic desideratum has a bearing on the evolution of the American Empire.

This truth was borne in on me last year because I happened then to be on the campus of the University of Peshawar in Western Pakistan. Pakistan, like the West Indian Confederation and the United Kingdom, is one of those allies of America's in whose territory the United States has acquired bases. I left Peshawar for visits to India and Afghanistan and returned to Peshawar to hear the news that Mr Kruschev had drawn a red ring round Peshawar on his bombing map. While I had been away, the U-2 had taken off from the so-called 'installation' a few miles to the south-west of Peshawar city. It is obvious that every American base on allied territory is a possible apple of discord between America and the allied country concerned—and each of America's allies is, of course, concerned one hundred per cent in the use made by America of her bases on that ally's territory. What may be at stake for each of America's allies is nothing less than the risk of being annihilated by Russia in retaliation for action that America may take.

This situation has raised a constitutional question. One

can make the point by parodying a famous slogan that was coined in America when things were boiling up towards America's Revolutionary War. If it was reasonable then for Great Britain's thirteen colonies to insist on 'no taxation without representation', 'no annihilation without representation' seems an even more reasonable demand for America's allies to present to America today. To be taxed without being given a say was provocative, but to be annihilated without being given a say would be intolerable. The U-2's sortie from the 'installation' at Peshawar last year has raised—and raised acutely and urgently—the question of who is to have the last word in taking political and military decisions which are literally matters of life and death for America's allies as well as for America. The seriousness of this constitutional issue is illustrated by the history of Rome's constitutional relations with her Italian allies—another episode in which we know how the story ended. Under a system of alliances between a paramount power and its satellites, Rome called the tune, but her Italian allies paid the piper. The allies protested; Rome turned a deaf ear. Eventually, the allies compelled Rome to give them a voice in her counsels; they compelled her to give them her citizenship. This was no more than justice, but the allies had to extort the concession from Rome by taking extreme measures. They did not win the Roman franchise till they had seceded from Rome and actually taken up arms against her.

As you will see, I am suggesting that America has acquired an empire and that, though this American Empire is today still in an early stage of its development, it has been evolving, in some respects, along the same lines as at least one of the notorious empires of the past. These suggestions of mine will, I know, be unpalatable to American minds. Their distastefulness is a good reason why you should consider these ideas, whether, on consideration, you reject or accept them. It is, I think, important for America to take a look at this picture of herself as an empire-builder, because anyone who appears to be building an empire inevitably incurs suspicion and unpopularity. This is happening today to America in her turn. But, all the same, this does not account for America's present ill-success in her competition with Russia. It does not, because Russia, too, has been building an empire; Russia, too, has been incurring the suspicion and unpopularity that every empire-builder brings upon himself; and the American way of empire-building has a saving grace which the Russian way lacks.

This saving grace of the American Empire is, indeed, one that is unprecedented in the history of empires and is a distinctive and characteristic American innovation. The American Empire that has come into existence since the Second World War is the first empire known to history in which the imperial power has paid, and paid voluntarily, for its dominant position instead of drawing financial profits from it. The nineteenth-century British Empire used to pride itself on the fact that it did not take tribute from its subjects. All the same, Great Britain did draw indirect profits from her empire in the shape of openings for British business and also in the shape of salaries and pensions for British colonial administrators. And most other imperial powers have taken advantage of their position to draw direct profits from it. By contrast, the United States made a new departure in the history of imperialism when she launched the Marshall Plan. America's ability to propose such a plan signified that the American Empire was by then an accomplished fact. At the same time it signified that America intended to make her imperial position felt by giving economic aid to the peoples under her ascendancy, instead of asserting herself by exploiting them economically in the traditional way.

What is more, America did not set this new standard of imperial morality just for herself alone. She established a precedent which all other surviving imperial powers have quickly found themselves obliged to adopt. Britain and France, for instance, are now paying heavily for the political privilege of still ruling those remnants of their former colonial empires that have not already attained independence. The Soviet Union, which plundered its East European satellites after the Second World War in a thoroughly old-fashioned way, is now heavily subsidizing China and is competing with the United States in giving economic aid to the uncommitted countries in Asia and Africa. Even Germany, who lost her former colonial empire in the First World War and failed to recover it in the Second, has publicly recognized that she has an obligation to share her postwar prosperity with the poorer countries of the World by contributing a German quota to the richer countries' foreign aid programmes. In fact, there has been a revolutionary change everywhere, since the Second World War, in the theory and practice of imperialism. This has been a novel revolution, and a beneficent one, in so far as it has converted imperialism into an instrument for redistributing wealth and so making the difference between wealth and poverty less extreme. This new world revolution, like the previous one, has been due to an American initiative. This is a fact that is well-known to all the World. So America's present ill-success in her competition with Russia for the World's good-will cannot be accounted for by this other well-known contemporary fact that the United States has been building an American Empire.

This new American Empire has at least two obvious and acknowledged merits which the older Russian Empire lacks. Its first merit is that it has come into existence against America's own will—in contrast to the usual eagerness of empire-builders to dominate their neighbours. The American Empire's second merit is one that we have just been noticing. America has been the first imperial power to give instead of taking; and, by setting this new precedent, America has constrained Russia and all other contemporary imperial powers to follow her example. When the World compares present-day American with present-day Russian imperial practice, the World's judgement unquestionably comes down in America's favour. There is, I should say, no doubt at all about this. But, if so, that only makes the present situation the more puzzling, because the World's judgement has not been reflected in the World's action. One would have expected that all third parties would have rallied round America for protection against Russia, and that Russia would have been left isolated and consequently

at a crushing disadvantage. Actually, the greatest of all
the third parties, namely China, has rallied, not to
America, but to Russia, though, in the past, China has
suffered severely from Russian imperialism, whereas she
has received from America valuable educational, economic, political, and military aid. Most of the other
independent Asian and African countries have held
aloof from America, though they have also held aloof
from Russia too. The only countries that have rallied
to the United States have been the other rich countries:
Canada, Australia, New Zealand, and the West European
states; and the rich are only a small minority of the
human race. Among the majority of mankind today,
America is not popular, and this is a paradox that needs
explaining.

I myself became sharply aware of this paradoxical
situation last spring and summer during a visit that I
was then paying to Western Pakistan and Afghanistan.
Along the Pakistan side of the frontier between Pakistan
and Afghanistan last June, I had opportunities of talking to a number of groups of local V.I.P.s. Most of these
were tribal chiefs, and most of them were very conservative-minded. In consequence, they were hostile to
Russia, and were much concerned over the possibility
that Russian influence might perhaps be spreading across
Afghanistan in their direction. What struck me particularly was that, in spite of this, they were hostile to
America too; and evidently they did not feel grateful
for American economic aid to their country. In my con-
versations with them, this subject was brought up more
than once (each time by the chiefs, not by me). The

tribal chiefs' line was that, when America made a loan to Pakistan, half the amount was swallowed up in fantastically high salaries for American executives. The pertinent point is not whether this allegation is true or false. The point is that these Pakistani tribesmen believed it, and that it had not been suggested to them by Communist propaganda, to which they were certainly immune.

In Afghanistan the paradox is still more striking. Why is Afghanistan today taking (as she apparently is) considerably more economic aid from the Soviet Union than from the United States? If Afghanistan had accepted economic aid from America, she could have done this without any political risk. Afghanistan is insulated from America by the Ocean and by Western Pakistan, and the Afghan Government must be well aware that the United States has no territorial ambitions in Asia. One would have expected Afghanistan to take, say, ninety per cent of the aid that she needs from America, while allocating ten per cent to the Soviet Union as a gesture of courtesy towards a powerful neighbour.

The Soviet Union is not only a powerful neighbour of Afghanistan's; she is also a formidable one. In the nineteenth century the Russian Empire advanced with giant strides up to Afghanistan's north-western frontier and beyond it. In 1885 the Russians occupied the Afghan district of Penjdeh, in spite of the efforts of Russia's nineteenth-century rival, Britain, to keep Russia's hands off Afghanistan. Today, Afghanistan has a common frontier with the Soviet Union that is hundreds of miles long. Neither the Afghans nor any of the rest of us believe that Russia has yet renounced her ambition to expand farther. No doubt it is unlikely that, in this Atomic Age, Russia will resort to the old-fashioned method of military conquest. But there is an alternative, namely 'peaceful penetration'. The Soviet Union will surely not refrain from continuing to expand by peaceful means if she finds opportunities, and economic aid is one obvious open sesame. The Afghan statesmen know this as well as anybody. Yet at this moment they seem to be allowing the Soviet Union to give their country the major part of the economic aid that she needs. They are doing this in spite of their suspicions of Russia's ultimate political intentions. These Afghan suspicions must be a serious handicap for Russia in the pursuit of her political designs in this quarter. Yet in Afghanistan Russia is apparently getting the better of America at the present time. This means that America must be labouring in Afghanistan under some handicap that is still greater than Russia's handicap there. What is this handicap of America's? Can we identify it? It is, I believe, the handicap of affluence.

Please have patience with me if, in this connexion, I venture to put to you again a point that I have made more than once already. This point may be trite, but it is certainly fundamental; so we cannot afford not to keep it in the foreground of our consciousness. My point is that affluence brings with it an automatic penalty. It inevitably insulates the rich minority from the poor majority of the human race. In a situation in which affluence is combined with some other insulator—with race-feeling or caste, for instance—the consequent degree of insulation may become very high.

This point has, I believe, always been an important one in human affairs, but it has become perhaps decisively important in the Atomic Age. The invention of the atomic weapon has not shocked us into becoming angels overnight. Even the fear of imminent annihilation cannot produce a sudden miraculous change in human nature. We are still divided against each other by conflicting interests, ideas, and ideals; we are still competing with each other; each of us is still bent on making his own will prevail over his neighbour's will. All the same, the Atomic Age has brought with it a change in the conditions under which mankind's age-old family quarrels are being carried on. The invention of the atomic weapon has put a premium on avoiding military action and on conducting our competition with each other by non-military means. In the Atomic Age, not military warfare but missionary warfare is the form that human competition is taking. This means competing for votes, and that means competing for the good-will of the mass of mankind. But good-will can be won only by fraternizing with the people whom one is seeking to win over. One cannot hope to touch their hearts unless one is able and willing to mix with them—to become one of them, in fact. And therefore, in a competition for the conversion of souls, a would-be missionary will be grievously handicapped by anything in his way of life and in his outlook that insulates him from the mass of mankind. Affluence and race-feeling are two formidable insulators. In combination they constitute a handicap that is great enough to ensure defeat if it is not overcome. America is now labouring under this crushing double handicap in her present competition with Russia for the good-will of the majority of the human race.

It is not very helpful to make this point in these general terms unless one goes on to illustrate one's thesis by concrete examples. So I am going to do this at my peril. But I will start by giving you some British illustrations. In my previous lecture I suggested that every mistake that America might be making today had been anticipated by my own country, and I proposed to draw

e time came. It has come now. If I

n's tail first, I shall feel less shy of

gle's feathers. The British lion and

re, no doubt, as different from each

l is from any bird. But, if we are to

historians, all forms of life have

ne original stock, so even creatures

ent from each other do have a

e American eagle's and the British

age is what Lewis Carroll calls

s'. I will give you my British ex-

Lahore, the second city of Western Pakistan. The most conspicuous monument in the centre of the city is 'the Club'. It is a massive building in the Greek style of architecture. By 1960 Pakistan had been independent for thirteen years; but still no Pakistani might set foot in the Club except as a Club servant—at least, so I was told by an Englishman who was living in Lahore at the time. Membership was confined to the local British business community; and a member might not even bring in a Pakistani with him as a guest. Now, for

Lahore write Philadelphia; transport that massive
Grecian building to a site across the street from Independence Hall; turn the clock back to the year 1796; and
then try to maintain the rule that membership of the
Club is to be confined to United Empire Loyalists who
have retained their British citizenship, and that no
American citizen who is not a Club servant may cross
the Club's threshold. Do you see the Philadelphians
tolerating that, thirteen years after the recognition of the
United States' independence by Great Britain? The Pakistanis do tolerate it at Lahore. This tolerance does them
honour, but the Club rule can hardly be fostering international good will. Before that Club fizzles out, its fantastic exclusiveness will have done a power of harm.

My first visit to the Indian subcontinent was in 1929.
I was staying with some English people in Bombay, on
Malabar Hill. At the time this was a close preserve for
British residents and Indian princes; so, on the first
morning, I walked down into the city to see what the
real Bombay was like. I prowled about and then rode
back in a bus, which, in any city, is one of the best ways
of seeing life. When my English hostess inquired what I
had been doing, and I came to the bus-ride, the temperature dropped fifty degrees. 'Went in a bus? You ought
to have hired a carriage.' I had been a traitor to the
Anglo-Saxon caste, and I had been reproved.

Here is another bus story. The hero of it is an old
English acquaintance of mine who happened to be a
member of a distinguished family. He was also a mon-
signore of the Roman Church. He lived and worked in
Rome and had the good sense to do his local travelling

by bus. One day an English lady and her daughter got on to the bus in which he was riding, and the girl sat down next to him. 'O my darling,' the mother exclaimed, 'don't sit so close to that nasty dirty Italian priest.' Monsignor Stanley raised his hat and addressed the mother. 'Madam,' he said, 'I *am* a priest, and I *may* be nasty, but I am *not* Italian, and I am *certainly* not dirty.' At the next stop the two Englishwomen fled. Serve them right.

In the nineteenth century there were English 'colonies', as they called themselves, in some of the most famous cities of Italy. These were composed of well-to-do English people who could afford to live abroad because they did not need to earn their living. They were attracted to Italy by her climate and her past, but not by any wish to make friends with living Italians. They dug themselves in on Italian ground, but they lived in a state of siege. They had their own English cooks, housemaids, doctors, clergymen, and artists. To bring their clergymen with them may have been pardonable, as they were Protestant residents in a Roman Catholic country. To bring foreign artists to Italy might seem like bringing coals to Newcastle. But, when once one starts insulating oneself from the natives and all their works, it is difficult to know where to stop. If one has convinced oneself that one would be poisoned if one ventured to taste Italian food or drink, one will fight shy of buying Italian pictures. It will be safer to employ a fellow-countryman to provide one with a drawing of the leaning tower of Pisa or a painting of the Roman campagna. Like chianti and macaroni, old masters might be unhygienic.

Well, now that I have given some British illustrations

of Anglo-Saxon attitudes, I shall feel less shy of supplementing these with some contemporary American parallels.

Since the Second World War there has been a revolutionary change in the representation of the United States abroad. America's earliest representatives in foreign parts were not diplomatists or consuls or commercial travellers; they were missionaries of the Christian religion. Of course, missionaries, like men and women in other walks of life, are not all perfect paragons. Yet, for the most part, these unofficial pioneers of American action outside America were men and women who had renounced opportunities for making money at home for the sake of devoting themselves to a disinterested mission. They were self-sacrificing; their material standard of living was low; and the barrier between them and the foreign peoples among whom they worked was therefore low proportionately. Since the Second World War the missionaries have been swamped by a host of official representatives, civilian and military. For instance, there is the personnel of the U.S. Air Force units at the bases leased by the United States from her allies; there is the personnel of the United States Information Service; and there are any number of teams of technicians. Today, America's official representatives abroad are legion. Yet I doubt whether they are proving as effective in winning esteem and good will for America as that handful of missionaries who were their nineteenth-century predecessors.

Those missionaries were, and are, dedicated souls; and dedication overcomes barriers. The barrier of affluence is overcome in the very act of embracing a missionary career. The barrier of race-feeling is overcome by the resolve to preach the Gospel to every creature. The barrier of home-sickness is overcome by the conviction that the missionary's work is worth the price of severe personal sacrifices. I once had the privilege of being present when a party of American missionaries, stationed in a remote corner of Manchuria, were bidding a long farewell to their wives and children. The mothers were taking the children home to be educated. It might be years before those American families were united again. It was such a moving scene that it is as vivid to me now as it was when I witnessed it thirty-one years ago. I was moved by the grief at parting and the fortitude with which it was borne. I was moved most of all by the faith which inspired those American families to endure that ordeal. No doubt, it would be unreasonable to expect anything like so high a standard of spiritual achievement from laymen whose foreign service is not a religious vocation but is merely a professional task. Yet, unless America's present-day governmental representatives abroad can catch some of the spirit of their predecessors the religious missionaries, I do not see how they can succeed in carrying out their own secular mission.

Homesickness is, I should say, a conspicuous and distinctive handicap of Americans outside America. On first thoughts one might have expected the Americans to be the last people in the World who would suffer seriously from this particular psychological malady. One might have assumed that every American would have been inoculated against homesickness by his family history. Every American now alive is descended from ancestors who plucked up their roots in the Old World—or had them plucked up for them—and struck new roots in North America at some date within the last three hundred and fifty-four years. Perhaps, however, it is precisely the tradition of this ancestral experience that makes present-day Americans sensitive to homesickness. Transplantation—even a more or less voluntary self-transplantation—is a severe ordeal for human nature. People who have experienced it may perhaps bequeath a traditional horror of it to their descendants. In any case, I think there can be no doubt that Americans are unusually prone to homesickness, whatever the explanation of this fact may be.

In England during the later years of the Second World War one was constantly meeting soldiers belonging to allied countries. Some came from Continental European countries that the Germans had temporarily occupied; others came from overseas, and by far the largest contingent of these overseas soldiers came from the United States. The Continental European soldiers—Norwegians, Dutch, Belgians, and French—had two psychological hardships to contend with. They had not only left their home countries; they had lost them and had been cut off from all communication with their families. They did not know when, if ever, they would recover their homes and be reunited with their wives and children. Their second handicap was that, in Fortress Britain, in which they were standing siege, the local language was a different one from their own. By contrast, the American soldiers in Britain could communicate in their own language with the natives; they were in touch with their families at home, and their home country was intact and uninvaded. All the same, it was the refugee non-English-speaking soldiers from Continental Europe who managed to make themselves more or less at home in Britain. The American soldiers were obvious expatriates all the time. From first to last they looked forlorn. The contrast was striking and paradoxical.

Since then, I have met this same homesickness among Americans stationed abroad under the easier conditions of peace-time. In the spring of 1959 I was doing some lecturing in West Germany under the auspices of U.S.I.S., and one day I found myself travelling from Bad Godesberg to Frankfurt in a U.S. Government car in company with the daughter of one of the American officials posted at Bad Godesberg who was on her way back to the American high school at Frankfurt after her usual week-end at home with her family. I myself had never been at school abroad, and I had been conscious of a consequent life-long handicap. I had never learnt to speak any foreign language properly. Thinking of the opportunity that my travelling companion was enjoying through having the luck to find herself at school in Germany, I asked her how many German girls there were in the school. 'Oh, there are some,' she said, 'but, of course, they all speak English.' As we approached Frankfurt, I asked the girl to direct the driver to her school, so that we could take her there before I went on to my own destination. She was, I should say, about seventeen years old, and she travelled by road between her school at Frankfurt and her temporary home at Bad Godesberg

every week-end. 'I don't know Frankfurt,' she said. 'But
I thought you had been at school here for the last year
or two.'—'Yes, I have. But we don't go into the city. We
just go from the school to the P.X. and back, and fortunately they are quite close to each other.' So we went
to the American consulate to ask the way, and in the
car-park there the girl suddenly became animated for
the first time. 'Oh, look at that,' she exclaimed. She was
pointing to the number-plate of one of the parked cars.
'Do you see that Washington, D.C., number-plate? That
almost makes me feel as if I were back home again.' This
poor girl's homesickness was preventing her from gain-
ing any benefit at all from living in a foreign country at
what would normally be an impressionable age. Her
psychological resistance to her foreign surroundings was
proving one hundred per cent effective.

The P.X., which was that American girl's life-line, is,
for that very reason, perhaps the biggest of the handicaps that America has imposed on herself in her conduct
of the cold war. For American expatriates, the P.X. is
like a honey-pot to bees; for the natives it is like a red
rag to a bull. The scent of the P.X. attracts homesick
Americans wives and mothers from hundreds of miles
away. One American mother, whose guest I was at Bad
Godesberg, spent the best part of a day driving her
children to the super-P.X. at Wiesbaden and back in
order to buy for her children canvas shoes that she
might have bought at a German store in Bad Godesberg
by just walking round the block. No doubt, this mother
was a victim of the American colony's self-insulation. If
her children had appeared at the American school in

Bad Godesberg in German shoes, they might have been
jeered at by the other children. All children, everywhere
and in all circumstances, are slaves to convention and are
merciless to any child who does not conform. But why
should there have been a separate American school at
Bad Godesberg? Why should not the American children
there have gone to one or other of the excellent native
schools in the town? If they had been allowed to profit by
this opportunity for having a German schooling, they
would have been furthering the purpose for which their
fathers had been posted in Germany. They would have
mastered the German language, have become at home
in the German way of life, and have made friends with
a number of their German contemporaries. In fact, they
would have become citizens of life-long value to their
own country, because they would have become so many
living links between America and one of the countries
for whose good-will the United States is competing with
the Soviet Union. America is missing this opportunity
for furthering her own purposes abroad, and she is taking
enormous pains to play Russia's game instead of her own.
She has built up for Americans abroad an elaborate and
effective self-insulating apparatus of schools, P.X.s, and
government hotels in which Americans abroad can continue to live just as if they were still inside the United
States.

My American hostess's shoe-buying expedition to the
super-P.X. at Wiesbaden had intrigued me so much that
I persuaded my host to take me there—that is, to take
me to the door, for an American P.X. is like the British
Club at Lahore: natives may not cross its threshold ex-

cept as employees; and, though I was not a German
native, I was a British one. Standing just outside that
door, I found myself in a key position for gauging the
prospects of the cold war. It really *was* like a bee-hive.
American wives and mothers were swarming in and out.
Taking my cue from the American girl in the car-park
at Frankfurt, I looked at the number-plates of the cars
parked in front of the super-P.X. at Wiesbaden. These
number-plates told me that some of the American ladies
had come from fantastically distant corners of West
Germany. The Wiesbaden P.X. was evidently their
Mecca. Scanning their faces, I found myself distressed
and concerned at what seemed to me to be the prevalent
expression. They looked worried, strained, resentful, and,
in extreme cases, almost savage. They were exiles who
were unreconciled to their lot. Evidently they had made
this pilgrimage to the super-P.X. in the pathetic hope of
finding solace and relief in this enclave of American
territory *in partibus peregrinorum*. But the actual effect
seemed to have been the opposite. Their homesickness
had been inflamed to an almost unbearable degree by
setting foot on this patch of American ground that the
P.X. represented for them. Fortunately, P.X.-bound
officials and their families are not America's only present-
day representatives abroad. There are also students and
other young people who travel for love and are ready to
live hard.

Buying American in a P.X. insulates the American
buyer from the natives whatever kind of consumer goods
she may be purchasing; but the insulating effect is most
extreme and most serious in the food and drink depart-

ment. Food and drink are not simply necessities of physical life. In human life they are also symbols of the eater's and drinker's attitude to her or his fellow human beings. Since time immemorial—perhaps since a time before our ancestors had become fully human—eating and drinking with somebody has been a token of entering into communion with him. It has been a ritual act signifying that one feels him to be one's fellow-creature. Conversely, refusing to eat and drink with someone is a declaration of apartheid. Self-insulation therefore produces peculiarly grave effects when it is carried into this field.

One day last March I was being hospitably entertained for lunch on the campus of the University of Peshawar by an American professor and his wife. The professor was one of a team that had been seconded from a particular university in the United States to this particular university in Pakistan for the laudable purpose of forging links of friendship between the two universities and, through these, between the two countries. The meal was an excellent one in the American style, and, half way through it, my hostess remarked on their good fortune in finding themselves posted within one hundred and ten miles of the P.X. at Rawal Pindi. 'Everything on this table comes from there,' she said. 'What, including the bread?'—'Well, not the bread, but the flour of which the bread is made. It is American flour, and the P.X. supplies even that to us.' That American housewife and her husband had no notion of the damage that they were doing, three times a day, to Pakistani-American relations. They did not suspect what was passing through the mind

of the English-speaking Pakistani bearer who was waiting on us, or of the versatile Pakistani cook behind the
scenes who had served us those American rations *à
l'Américaine.*

I did know what those Pakistanis were feeling, because
my wife and I had once had the same experience at home
in England. During a visit to the United States we had
rented our house in London to a young American doctor
and his wife. They had come over on a Fulbright fellowship. The doctor was going to study in London the
English practice of a particular branch of medical
science. Before we left, my wife gave the doctor's wife a
list of the local shops which she had found the best: the
butcher, baker, grocer, greengrocer, fishmonger, fruiterer,
dairy, and the rest. (In London we do not go in much for
super-markets.) When we came home and took over our
house again, we found that the doctor's wife had never
once made use of my wife's shopping guide. She and her
husband had bought everything that they had eaten and
drunk in London at the P.X. in the United States
Embassy there. He was a doctor; they had a small baby;
they were taking no chances with the local food and
drink. So they had thrown away the opportunity of
getting to know something of the local life of the country
that they were visiting. They had been living, in fact, in
a state of siege, like the members of those nineteenth-
century English 'colonies' in Florence and Rome. My
wife and I found ourselves surprised at the liveliness of
our reaction. I do not think we are touchy above the
average, and I am really sure that we are not chauvinistic.
Yet we found ourselves decidedly piqued both as indi-

viduals and as English people. The assumption that our native food and drink was poison got under our skins.

I had the same experience again this year in India. On more than one occasion an Indian professor who was showing me the greatest consideration made the most far-fetched excuses to avoid eating with me under the eyes of his fellow Hindus. These Indian professors were Brahmans; I, of course, was an outcaste; and for them to eat with me in public would have stamped them as unclean, not hygienically, but ritually. In this case I was not annoyed but was amused—I suppose because my Brahman professional colleagues were patently embarrassed at treating me as Hindu custom demanded, and also because their subterfuges were transparent. But the point is that their behaviour had the same self-insulating effect as my American tenants' behaviour had had. Anglo-Saxon attitudes are not a British and American monopoly; they are also characteristic of Afrikaners, Germans, and high-caste Hindus. Fortunately these self-insulators, even in the aggregate, are only a small cranky minority of the human race. The Muslims and the Spanish-speaking and Portuguese-speaking Roman Catholic Christians are more typical. These spiritual pioneers will not only eat and drink with their native converts. They will inter-marry with them. God bless them. If the human race does now at last succeed in coalescing into a single family, the credit will be theirs, not ours.

III

CAN AMERICA RE-JOIN HER OWN REVOLUTION?

MY first lecture in this series was historical; my second was critical; so I have put myself under a moral obligation to try to make this third and last lecture constructive. Can America re-join her own revolution? That is my subject today. Can America throw off the handicap of affluence? Or, short of that, can she hope for some lucky turn of affairs that might compensate for this handicap without requiring America to get rid of it? This second question is the link between my previous lecture and the present one.

Can America reasonably hope to see her handicap neutralized by Russia's following America's lead? Is Russia likely to saddle herself with the same handicap in her turn? Russia is certainly doing her utmost to overtake and, if possible, surpass America in material achievement, i.e., in the production of material wealth. And, no doubt, Russia would have sacrificed her present advantage over America in the waging of the cold war if, one day, the average personal affluence, measured in terms of the personal possession of consumer goods, were to become greater in the Soviet Union than in the United States. Can America look forward to seeing her rival come to her rescue in this obliging way? If there is any prospect of this happening, it is, I am afraid, a faint one.

It is not, of course, inconceivable that the Soviet Union's aggregate national income might come to exceed that of the United States. No doubt, an ideology of any kind—collectivist or individualist—puts a brake on productivity; but the uneconomic effect of the Communist ideology might turn out to be less restrictive than that of the Free Enterprise ideology. Yet, even in that event, it seems improbable that anything like so large a proportion of the Soviet Union's productive power would ever be allocated to the provision of consumer goods for personal use as has now become the rule in the United States and in other Western countries to a hardly lesser degree.

It is not just that the Soviet Government would be likely to give priority to other ways of using the national product. I do not believe that the Russian people themselves would ever be likely to crave for the personal possession of consumer goods on the present-day American scale. No doubt, the Russians today would like to possess a considerably larger quota of consumer goods per head than has come their way so far. But there is a limit, and a narrow one, to the quantity of goods that can be effectively possessed, in the sense of being genuinely enjoyed, by a single human being in a single lifetime. I became aware of this truth at a stage in my own life at which I happened to have a personal connexion with an English family that had great hereditary possessions. I then discovered that, when a human being is the legal possessor of a palace, the palace actually owns its nominal possessor. He becomes, in effect, the janitor of property that is too vast for him ever to be able to make it his

own in a personal sense. A human being's capacity for
effectively owning material possessions is small. If he has
a yearning for the infinite, this can find an outlet only in
the spiritual dimension—in the realms of knowledge,
art, and, perhaps above all, religion. This is true not just
of Russian human nature; it is equally true, I am sure,
of human nature in general, including American human
nature. Professor Galbraith has pointed out that the
present-day scale of personal consumption in America
is a long way in excess of people's genuine personal
wants. The measure of the difference, in the United
States, between genuine wants and actual consumption is
given by the scale of the wants-manufacturing industry
that is carried on today on Madison Avenue. I do not
believe that either Russia or any other country outside
the United States will ever saddle itself with a Madison
Avenue or even hanker after this form of psychological
slavery. It is surely much more likely that there will be
a revolt against Madison Avenue one day in America
itself. After all, one of the most precious of America's
lost human freedoms is the freedom from the tyranny
of advertising.

For these reasons I suggest that it would be rash for
America to expect Russia to come to her rescue by taking
America's present handicap of affluence on her own
shoulders. I do not think that Russia is likely to make
this mistake. So this handicap seems likely to remain
the monopoly of America and the other Western countries, and therefore to remain our peculiar problem.
This handicap is indeed a formidable one if I have been
right in suggesting, as I did in the preceding lecture,

that it does not merely insulate but alienates. I have sometimes heard American friends of mine cite the present-day unparalleled average amount of personal property per head in the United States as evidence that the American economic and social system is pre-eminently excellent. If this is the judgement of some Americans, it is, I believe, a minority judgement if we take the human race as a whole into account. Travelling about the World, as I have been doing rather actively during the last few years, I have got the impression that the present American standard of material living is not admired or envied by mankind at large. This standard is, of course, beyond the horizon of the very great majority of living human beings. The great majority needs no Madison Avenue to impose unwanted demands on it; and a contingent, even though a small one, of this majority consists of the indigent minority of American citizens that co-exists with the affluent majority in the United States. The wants of the indigent mass of mankind, whether inside the United States or outside it, are clamant and urgent. In Asia and Africa, this majority wants the next meal for the family; it wants some palm-leaf thatching to shelter it from the monsoon rains; it wants a piece of cotton cloth to clothe the family's nakedness. A small minority of this great majority of mankind will have additional genuine wants beyond these elementary wants; and, for this minority, the American standard of material living might perhaps have some intelligible meaning. Yet, even if this handful of relatively affluent non-Westerners were fully cognizant of the American standard of living, I do not believe they

would covet it for themselves. To take upon themselves
the burden of obeying Madison Avenue's commandments might well seem to them to be as heavy a yoke
as submitting, let us say, to the laws of Moses or
Zarathustra.

If I am right about this, America cannot afford to sit
pretty in the hope that her competitors will take her
self-imposed handicaps upon themselves. America will
have to break down the barriers that her affluence has
raised between her and the World's ordinary non-affluent
people—the great poor majority of mankind. I had been
wondering whether it might not be possible for America's
present-day secular representatives abroad to take a leaf
out of the nineteenth-century missionaries' book when
I read in the newspapers about President Kennedy's idea
of doing this very thing. I was excited by this piece of
news, and was still more excited when, a few weeks later,
the idea of the Peace Corps was put into action. Critics
of the present Administration have, of course, been
quick to point out various ways in which this project
might miscarry. Yet the risk involved in launching it is,
I should say, a small one compared to the risk of taking
no action in this field. Inaction here, would, I believe,
mean eventually losing the cold war. On the other hand,
if the Peace Corps makes even a partial success of its job,
it may achieve for America, and for the Western World
as a whole, the one thing that we need above all. It may
help us to break down the psychological barrier that now
insulates us from the great majority of the human race.
The enthusiasm with which the launching of the Peace
Corps has been welcomed is therefore cheering. The

organizers of the Peace Corps already have an abundant reservoir of volunteers from whom they can recruit a carefully chosen band.

The standard has to be a high one; for this is to be a band of young American men and women who will be prepared to dedicate themselves to the work of representing America abroad, and who will also be prepared to make the personal sacrifices that will be required of them if they are to do the job effectively. These sacrifices will be greater than those required of the members of the armed forces in peace-time. What the members of the Peace Corps will need to do first of all, as a preliminary to doing anything else, is to lower their standard of material living from the present customary American level. They will have to bring it down near enough to the local level, in the country in which they are posted, to make it possible for them to mix freely and easily with the natives. If these new American lay missionaries can achieve this, then, for the first time since the beginning of the cold war, the United States will have representatives abroad who will be in a position to compete with their Russian opposite numbers on equal terms.

The test of success in this competition is to become invisible. I became aware of this point last spring when I was travelling in Afghanistan, which is one of the most active theatres of the cold war. In Afghanistan today an American or any other Westerner is not only visible but conspicuous. He does not wear the local clothes or eat the local food; he does not do his travelling on foot or even on donkey-back. I myself was travelling round Afghanistan in this conspicuous way for twenty-three days, and I was five weeks in the country altogether. But, in all that time, I never once set eyes on a Russian for certain, though I was made aware of the Russians' presence by seeing the results of Russian activities. For instance, the Russian bread baked in Kabul (this Russian bread is made of local flour) and the Russian tunnel that was being driven under one of the passes over the Hindu Kush.

I tried to account for this to myself by assuming that the Russians were taking advantage of a facility for making themselves invisible which was at their disposal if they had chosen to use it. The political frontier between the Soviet Union and Afghanistan is not also an ethnic one. At least two local nationalities, the Uzbegs and the Tajiks, straddle this frontier. So I imagined to myself that the Soviet Government must be employing Uzbeg and Tajik citizens of the Soviet Union to do its work for it in Afghanistan, and that some of the obvious Uzbegs and Tajiks whom I had been passing on the road in Afghanistan must have been Soviet citizens in Soviet employment there. Afterwards, however, I was told, on what I believe was good authority, that, on Soviet jobs in Afghanistan, the employment of Soviet Uzbegs and Tajiks is ruled out by agreement between the two Governments. The Russians do not care to let loose their local Asian citizens among these peoples' kinsmen in Afghanistan, while the Afghans, on their side, do not want the Soviet Union to be represented in Afghanistan by people who would be difficult for the Afghan Government to keep under observation because they would be indistinguishable from its own Uzbeg and Tajik subjects. Apparently the invisible representatives of the Soviet Union in Afghanistan are not local Soviet Asians but are authentic Russians. And, if that is the truth, their achievement of invisibility is a remarkable feat. In spite of their being Russians, they must be dressing, eating, and travelling in the Afghan way. They must, in fact, have made themselves at home in Afghanistan on the country's own terms. Here we have the standard that President Kennedy's American lay missionaries will have to live up to spiritually—that is to say, live down to physically—if they are to produce the result that is being expected of them.

They can be asked to live hard; but, unlike the missionaries of a religion and unlike soldiers on active service, they can hardly be asked to be heroes. In the preceding lecture I mentioned the heroism of some American missionaries in Manchuria. These missionaries and their families were willing to endure the grief of a long separation for the sake of carrying out their mission. A soldier's mission may require him deliberately to sacrifice his life, and this not only by exposing himself as a target for shells and bullets. At a critical stage of the campaign in 'Iraq in the First World War, an officer—his name was General Maude—did deliberately sacrifice his life by drinking a cup of cold water. There was a local epidemic of cholera; to drink unboiled water was certain death; and a tribal chief, whose adherence might just tip the balance in the competition for the command of 'Iraq, greeted General Maude with a cup of water which he offered to him as a token of fellowship and alliance. If the general had left the water untasted, he would have saved his own life at the cost of mortally offending an indispensable ally. So he drained the cup unhesitatingly and duly died of the deadly draft. Such heroism as that is not, of course, called for on any but supremely critical occasions. I should not have blamed my American host and hostess in Peshawar or my American tenants in London for drawing water for themselves and their families exclusively from a P.X. if the native water had been deadly. The members of the Peace Corps cannot and need not be asked to live up to General Maude's war-time standard. It will be enough if they can manage to swallow down some English warm beer or some Afghan kebabs and pilaf. If they go even to those moderate lengths of self-mortification, they will reap a harvest of good will for their country at the price of only a moderate amount of personal discomfort for themselves.

When America's new lay missionary army has been recruited and has been put into the field, it may be expected that it will act as a powerful leaven on the mass of America's expatriated government officials and technicians. The veterans will surely catch something of the new spirit of the recruits. It is greatly to be hoped that they will, for the only alternative remedy would be the difficult one of drastically thinning the ranks of America's present official representatives abroad. This could be done by taking a leaf out of the Book of Judges. Do you remember how Gideon reduced the numbers of his army from thirty-two thousand to three hundred? If you have forgotten, re-read Judges, Chapter 7, verses 1-7. The last of a series of thinning operations was a drinking test. 'The Lord said unto Gideon: Every one that lappeth of the water with his tongue, as a dog lappeth, him shalt thou set by himself; likewise every one that boweth down upon his knees to drink. And the number of them that lapped . . . were three hundred men, but all the rest of the people bowed down upon their knees to drink water. And the Lord said unto Gideon: By the three hundred men that lapped will I save you, and deliver the Midianites into thine hand; and let all the other people go every man unto his place.'

The President could produce Gideon's result by two strokes of the pen. He would simply have to sign one executive order abolishing all P.X.s throughout the World, and another executive order releasing from their contracts all American government servants abroad who feel incapable of lapping up the local food and drink. This test would be likely to thin out the ranks of the warriors almost as drastically as Gideon's test did. Gideon finally reduced his army from thirty-two thousand men to three hundred. President Kennedy could not reduce his on anything approaching that scale. All the same, a hardy remnant does sometimes make a more efficient task-force than the host from which it has been picked out. A representative abroad who cannot do without a P.X. is not a political asset; he is a political liability. He is bringing unpopularity upon his country instead of winning for it the good will that was his government's objective in posting him abroad.

Perhaps he might become a political asset to his country if he were to transfer his custom from the local P.X. to the local native stores. The natives' prosperity would be increased through the purchase, by Americans stationed abroad, of native food, drink, and other consumer goods on what, by native standards, is the lavish scale of the American standard of living. And this increase in the natives' prosperity would bring popularity to the American purchasers and to their country. But of course this way of dealing with America's political problem abroad would aggravate America's economic problem of redressing her present adverse balance of payments. Suggestions have been made for coping with this economic problem by aggravating the political one. On the 4th February of this year 1961, for instance, *The Philadelphia Inquirer* published, under the headline 'Keep Guard up against Inflation', an editorial on President Kennedy's first batch of economic and financial proposals which contained the following passage:

'Mr Kennedy's directive calling for reduced expenditures by U.S. servicemen and their dependents in foreign countries is one practical way to check the flow of gold from this country. We would suggest, as a further step, that the servicemen and dependents be encouraged to increase buying of American goods. Military personnel and their families stationed abroad constitute a ready-made "foreign market" for American exporters to cultivate.'

I venture to put it to you that this suggestion is not an improvement on President Kennedy's directive. The President's directive asks Americans abroad to spend less, without asking them not to make their purchases in native stores. Where they buy, not how much they buy, is what makes Americans abroad popular or unpopular, as the case may be. If they buy native goods, this will be appreciated, even if their purchases are reduced to the modest scale of the natives' own purchases. So the President's directive can be doubly advantageous for America. It is to America's advantage politically as well as economically. Besides helping her to reduce her adverse balance of payments, it can help her to lower the psychological barrier between Americans serving abroad and the natives of the countries in which they are posted. For the height of this barrier is proportionate, as we have seen, to the difference between the two parties' respective material standards of living and to the degree of the expatriated Americans' self-insulation. On the other hand, *The Inquirer's* proposal to increase the degree of self-insulation would raise the barrier to a still greater height, and would thereby increase the unpopularity of Americans in the countries whose good will America is seeking to win.

When one is raising an army it pays to set oneself a high standard for the selection of one's recruits. This pays whether the army that one is raising is a military force of the traditional kind or whether it is a new model Peace Corps whose assignment is to wage a missionary war. There are two qualifications that are indispensable if the chosen few are to be winners. First, they must be sincere and disinterested and whole-hearted in dedicating themselves to their mission; second, they must enjoy it. They must undertake it, not as an onerous duty, but as a thrilling adventure. In other words, they must embrace poverty in the spirit in which it was embraced by Saint Francis of Assisi. You see, I am asking for a very high standard. Saint Francis is the greatest soul that has appeared in our Western World so far since our Western Civilization came up out of the Dark Ages. Yet Saint Francis's standard is not higher than what is needed for this enterprise. It is, in fact, exactly what we do need in our present crisis. Quite a small band of Franciscan-minded representatives of the United States abroad might succeed, I believe, in turning the tide of the cold war in the Western World's favour.

As I have said, this is a big thing to ask for, but it is not an impossible thing to obtain. A few people of this kind—by 'this kind' I mean the salt of the earth—are to be found everywhere and at all times. But, supposing that America can find a dedicated company of Franciscan-minded Americans to serve her as representatives abroad, it will not be enough for the nation just to commission them and then sit back. The operative word here is the word 'representatives'. The representation of America is the purpose for which these men and women are being recruited and posted; and a representative is worse than useless if he is not a fair sample of the party that he represents. If the people who have sent him abroad to represent them do not share the ideals for which their representative stands, if they do not live the kind of life that their representative's ideals inspire their representative to live, this will quickly become apparent to the people among whom their representative is working. This discrepancy between the representative and his fellow-countrymen at home will cause scandal and disillusionment. And the finer a person the representative is, and the greater the gulf between his ideals and conduct and those of the mass of his fellow-countrymen, the greater the scandal and the disillusionment abroad is likely to be. Therefore the posting of a new kind of representative abroad carries with it a commitment on the home front. It commits a country to reconsidering its ideals and perhaps revising its way of life at home to bring these into line with its new representation abroad. The sample must be a fair sample; the façade must be all of a piece with the building. America's present representation abroad is perhaps a fair sample of the American people in its recent mood. The P.X., and the importance of its role in the life of Americans now expatriated on government service, is evidence, I should say, that America's present representation abroad has been truly representative. But then America's present representation abroad is in danger of losing the cold war for America, if I have not been entirely wrong in my train of argument up to this point. Anyway, if you will concede, for the sake of the argument, that America's representation abroad does need changing in character in order to save America from losing the cold war, this leads us to the American application of the point that I am now making. My point is that, if one decides to change the character of one's representation, one is committing oneself to changing one's own character to match. If, at present, America's victory in the cold war abroad is in doubt, as I believe it is, this means that the American way of life on the home front is now in question; it means that the American way of life is due for a check-up—and this applies not just to the American way of life; it applies to the whole Western way of life in all

Western countries; for, by contrast with the rest of the World, all Western countries have 'gone American' in various degrees.

You see, the challenge of the cold war has brought us up against a very searching question : What is our purpose in life in America? What is our purpose in life in the Western World as a whole? And we cannot discuss, and, *a fortiori*, cannot answer, this question just in our own provincial terms. We have to consider the question in terms of mankind as a whole. The question is : What is the true end of Man? And this not just an economic question or a political one. It is also a religious question. It is, in fact, the first of the questions that are asked in the Scottish Catechism.

Let us begin with a negative definition of the true end of Man. The true end of Man is *not* to possess the maximum amount of consumer goods per head. When we are considering the demand for consumer goods, we have to distinguish between three things : our needs, our wants, and the unwanted demand, in excess of our genuine wants, that we allow the advertising trade to bully us into demanding if we are both rich enough and foolish enough to let ourselves be influenced by advertisements.

By our needs, I mean the minimum amount of material requirements—food, clothes, housing—without which we cannot remain alive. These needs are necessities óf life, but they are not the end for which life is lived. They are merely a means to that end. The means are physical, but the end is not. The end of human life is spiritual, and this spiritual purpose is what distinguishes Man from his non-human fellow living crea-

tures on the face of this planet. Some physical means
are, of course, indispensable for the pursuit of spiritual
ends because they are necessary for life itself. But,
measured in terms of quantity of consumer goods, the
material necessities of life add up to only a very modest
amount. See how Christian monks or Buddhist monks
live. This will give you a fair measure of what the
genuine necessities of life truly amount to. See how a
family of Indian peasants live. This will remind you
that, today, two-thirds or three-quarters of the human
race are still living at a level only just above the bare
minimum, and are sometimes falling below it.

By our wants I mean the wants that we become aware
of spontaneously, without having to be told by Madison
Avenue that we want something that we should never
have thought of wanting if we had been left in peace to
find out our wants for ourselves. Our wants include our
needs, of course, but they also include many times that
minimum amount of consumer goods and services. (At
the moment I am talking, as you will realize, of material
wants, not of spiritual wants.) Our wants are vastly
greater than our needs, even when our wants are not
inflated by the artificial stimuli of advertising agencies.
All the historic higher religions warn us to go slow in
seeking satisfaction for those of our wants that are surplus to our needs—even if these surplus wants happen
to be innocent in themselves. The religions warn us
against excessive self-indulgence in the satisfaction of
our material wants because they hold, and rightly hold,
that this is an obstacle to attaining the true end of Man
—the true end of Man being the pursuit of spiritual aims.

The religions give us this warning for our own sakes; but, of course, they are not concerned with just each one of us by himself, and no one of us can be concerned just with himself either. 'No man liveth unto himself and no man dieth unto himself.' Man is a social creature, and, as such, he has to take account, not only of his own needs and wants, but also of his neighbour's. So long as my neighbour's needs remain unsatisfied, it is my social and moral duty to supply his needs at the expense of my surplus wants. On this point the religions do not merely warn us; they exhort us and even command us. One of the basic commandments of all the religions is the commandment to give to the poor; and, in our present-day world this commandment is directed especially towards the Western minority of the human race. This Western minority is, at present, the rich minority. We have to share our surplus goods with the poor two-thirds or three-quarters of mankind. Among the Western peoples since the Second World War, America has taken the lead in recognizing this moral duty and in acting on it. The first step in this action was the launching of the Marshall Plan; but we shall have to go to much greater lengths than that—perhaps to greater lengths than any that we have yet dreamed of.

Where are we to make a beginning in this further advance along the road towards social justice? The rich nations today are squandering a very large part of their surplus product on rival armaments. If we could limit, reduce, or, best of all, abolish all armaments, conventional as well as atomic, we could release a vast amount of productive power in the Western countries and in the

Soviet Union for meeting the needs of the poor majority of mankind. No doubt, this would require a large and therefore difficult readjustment of the internal economic structure of the disarming countries. But statesmanship and technology are equal to that job. In two world wars they have already twice demonstrated their ability to harness the economy to new tasks when the motive for making the effort is sufficiently strong; and it is surely strong enough, now again, today. Our present crisis is as compelling as any world war fought with pre-atomic weapons. Moreover, if disarmament could be achieved, this would bring benefits to both sections of the human race. It would relieve the rich nations of their present fear, and the poor nations of their present want. However, disarmament requires agreement, and we know how difficult it is going to be to reach this. I believe that the nations and governments involved in the present armaments competition do sincerely want disarmament. What holds them back is not unwillingness; it is mutual suspicion and fear. Anyway, whatever the hindrance may be, we cannot count on disarmament to do what we want for us within any foreseeable period of time. So we must look elsewhere if we are looking for a quick release of Western productive power for employment on the urgent enterprise of satisfying the needs of the poor.

If we leave the possibility of disarmament out of the picture for present purposes, the first obvious field for retrenchment is the field of bogus wants—wants that are bogus in the sense that they would never have occurred to our minds if they had not been dinned into our ears by advertising agencies whose job is to enable manufacturers to unload on us unwanted goods. This whole sector of domestic consumption could be released for foreign aid by private initiative, without any need for government action. We have merely to do to ourselves what Odysseus did to his crew when they came within range of the Sirens' voices. Odysseus stopped up his sailors' ears with wax; so those Siren voices fell on deaf ears. We have merely to stop listening to Madison Avenue, and within a few weeks the whole advertising industry would collapse and would be liquidated. All the same, considering the infirmity of human purpose, I dare say private initiative might be glad of the help of governmental action, even though this might not be strictly indispensable. I do not know whether a stroke of the Presidential pen could abolish the advertising industry at home as well as the P.X.s abroad. If this were constitutionally possible, it would be an expeditious way of carrying out a most desirable piece of social reform that is long overdue in all Western countries. If the President's constitutional powers do not run to that, then, I suppose, we should have to ask the Congress to legislate the advertising industry out of existence.

Even when we have transferred productive power from catering for bogus wants of the Western minority to supplying genuine needs of the non-affluent majority of mankind, the transfer of wealth might turn out not to have been extensive enough to meet even the minimal material needs of the majority. But there would still be a further fund to draw on—the huge fund of those material wants of ours that are genuine but not essential. To draw on this fund would mean making calls on the religious virtue of self-denial for the sake of providing necessities of life for our fellow human beings. This virtue is enjoined upon us by all the historic religions with one voice. Judaism, Christianity, Islam, Zoroastrianism, Hinduism, Buddhism: they all call upon us to give to the poor. This is the action on the home front that would bring the home front into line with the standards of a Franciscan-minded band of lay missionaries in the foreign mission field. I am not suggesting that, on either front, self-sacrifice should necessarily be carried to heroic lengths. The American people is notoriously generous by temperament and by tradition. Give free rein to your American impulse to be generous, go on setting this American example to the other Western countries, and then we can feel fairly confident that the Western World as a whole will do for the rest of mankind what it is called upon to do by the voice of religion.

If America can bring herself to go this far, she will, I believe, have worked her passage back to a point at which it will become possible for her to rejoin her own revolution. The American Revolution was a truly glorious revolution. It was glorious for two reasons. The basic issues that it raised were spiritual, not material; and, even if this may not have been the intention of some of the Founding Fathers, it was in effect, as Jefferson perceived and Emerson proclaimed, a revolution for the whole human race, not just for the people of the Thirteen Colonies. The shot fired beside the bridge at Concord was not only heard round the World; it was taken as a signal, given to the World by the embattled American farmers, that the World Revolution had begun. On the surface, the American Revolution was concerned with politics: taxation and representation. Even as long ago as that, people got excited about taxation. The rate of the taxation that was a burning question in the seventeen-sixties and seventeen-seventies would seem unbelievably moderate nowadays; but, of course, the issue was not the rate, it was the principle; and the principle was the question of human rights. The American Revolution was glorious because it staked out human rights, and staked them out for all men.

Though I am a foreigner, I can tell you what was *not* one of the aims of the American Revolution. It was not its aim to provide the people of the Thirteen Colonies with the maximum amount of consumer goods per head. America's present affluence was not dreamed of by the Founding Fathers, and it was not one of their objectives. It has been the unplanned consequence of a marriage between the American people's human energy and the previously untapped non-human natural resources of the North American Continent. This affluence has been the reward of material achievement. It is a reward that is pleasant to the taste. At the same time, it has brought a penalty with it, as most material rewards do. It has side-tracked America from the main line of her own revolution, and it has insulated her from the rest of the human race. The American Revolution has gone thundering on. Nothing can stop it, no, not even the American hands that first set it rolling. But, during these last forty-four years, your revolution has gone ahead without you. The leadership has fallen into other hands. These non-American hands could never have seized the leadership of your revolution if you had not dropped it.

This penalty that you have been paying for your affluence is a heavy one. It is now threatening America's security, but it is also doing America graver harm than that. Affluence is estranging America from her own ideals. It is pushing her into the position of being the leader of the very opposite of what America's World Revolution stands for. It is pushing her into becoming the policeman standing guard over vested interests. But the future is still open. Your role in the coming chapter of the World's history is not yet irrevocably decided. It is still within your power to re-enter into your heritage. It is still within your power to re-capture the lead in your own revolution. I believe you will do it; for I do not believe that, when America is confronted with the choice, she will be willing to sell her revolutionary birthright for even a king-size mess of potage. I do not believe that she will submit to being the prisoner of her great possessions, like the young man who went away sorrowful.

America's destiny matters to America; the West's destiny matters to the West. But the destinies of both America and the West as a whole are of small importance by comparison with the destiny of the human race. What is the human race heading towards? That is the question.

Since Man became human, he has always been infinitely rich in spiritual potentialities. But, in order to realize these spiritual possibilities of his, he must have effective provision for his minimal material needs; and, in terms of material goods, Man has been paralysingly

poor till only the other day. The fabled wealth of Ormuz
and of Ind was the monopoly of a tiny privileged
minority: Great Moguls and Pharaohs and the like. It
is only within our own life-time that affluence has anywhere become the normal lot of the ordinary members
of a community. And, so far, this escape from our im-
memorially old poverty has been achieved only by a few
peoples, the Western peoples, out of all the peoples of
the World.

When starving people light upon a feast, they are apt
to glut themselves. Sometimes they even glut themselves
to death by over-loading a long-empty stomach with
more than it can digest. The starving man's gluttony is
human, but it is not edifying, and therefore it is not
satisfying either. It is no wonder that the peoples who
have been the first to attain to affluence should have
been tempted, in the first generation, to surfeit themselves with consumer goods. I fancy that future generations in the West will look back on this episode of
Western history with astonishment mingled with disgust. They may even feel some shame at being impli-
cated in our excesses through being our physical descendants. I feel sure that they will have grown tired, long
since, of being cluttered up with an immoderate amount
of material possessions. Through trial and error, they
will have discovered what is the optimum amount of
material possessions per head. By 'optimum' I mean the
amount that will give the human spirit the fullest opportunity to spread its wings and soar aloft. This, I believe,
is the American Revolution's true goal; and, whatever
America now does or does not do, I believe mankind

as a whole is going to strive to reach this goal, now that the glorious American Revolution has brought this goal within mankind's horizon.

The American Revolution has made a declaration of the spiritual rights of Man. But this American shot would not have been heard round the World if the charge of powder had not been a mighty one. What is this mighty force that has sent that sound rolling round and round the circumference of the planet? The impetus behind the American Revolution is the spirit of Christianity; the sound is the voice of God which speaks not only through Christianity but through all the historic religions which have preached their gospels to all the World and which, between them, have reached almost the whole of mankind. In the future, as in the past, the common spiritual essence of the historic religions will, I believe, be mankind's guiding light. When the ideologies have evaporated, and when Man's long unsatisfied hunger for material possessions has been appeased, and when Man has also been cured of his temporary gluttony by satiety, then, I believe, the ideals and the precepts that are embodied in the historic religions will come into their own at last.

What, then, is America's relation to the World Revolution? It is her revolution; it was she who launched it by firing that shot heard round the World. What about America's recently acquired affluence? It is a handicap, and a formidable one, but it is a handicap that can be overcome. Can America rejoin her own revolution? In my belief, this is still within her power. America's destiny is, I believe, still in America's own hands.

THE ECONOMY OF
THE WESTERN HEMISPHERE

I

THE WESTERN HEMISPHERE
IN A CHANGING WORLD

'THE Economy of the Western Hemisphere' is the subject
that the University of Puerto Rico and the Weatherhead
Foundation have chosen for me to introduce in these lectures, and for this group of distinguished scholars to discuss.
The University and the Foundation have shown us consideration in setting limits to our field. Even so, the limits
set for us are wide. All the same, I am going to begin by
trespassing beyond these limits. I find myself compelled to
do this by the changes that the World is undergoing in our
time. As I see it, it is now no longer possible to deal with
economics in insulation from other facets of human life, or
to deal with either hemisphere in isolation from the rest of
the surface of the globe. The chapter of mankind's history
on which we have now entered is one that is global in every
sense. To try to study it globally is, no doubt, a formidable
intellectual task. Yet, if we try to lighten this task by carving
up the indivisible reality of human affairs into artificial com-
partments, we shall be simplifying our picture at the cost of
distorting it, and this is too high a price to pay.

All over the World today there is a tension between the
requirements of economic efficiency and the demands of
social justice. This is surely the essence of the present
economic situation in Latin America. I believe it is also latent
in the economic situation in the United States. To attempt to
look at economics *in vacuo*, apart from their crucial inter-

play with social justice, would be unilluminating, because it would be unrealistic.

It would also be unrealistic to attempt to look at the Western Hemisphere today apart from its economic, military, political, and ethical relations with the rest of the World.

For nearly a century now, there has been a world market for Latin American products, mineral and agricultural. The world price of these products is vitally important to the Latin American peoples, because their income from the sale of these products abroad is virtually their sole means of payment for imports that have become an indispensable element in their economy. As we know, the world prices of primary products fluctuate, and these fluctuations have sometimes had disastrous effects on the economy, and consequently on the social and political life, of the exporting countries. Since the principal customer for the primary products of the tropical Latin American countries is the United States, these countries have been pressing the United States to co-operate with them in trying to stabilize the prices of their key primary exports. Until recently, at any rate, the United States has been unwilling to take up this Latin American suggestion, and the existence of a world market has been the United States' main argument for maintaining this negative attitude on a question that is of such great concern to the United States' Latin American associates. This United States answer may or may not be an adequate one. I shall touch on this question again in my next lecture. At the moment, I am simply making the point that there is, in fact, a world market, and that its existence does affect intra-Western-Hemisphere commercial relations.

The whole World has been a single market for some key commodities since the second half of the nineteenth century. Since 1948, when the atomic weapon was acquired by the

Soviet Union in succession to the United States, the whole World has also become a single slaughter-house. Today, a bomb with an atomic war-head could be delivered from any point on or above the Earth's surface, or in adjoining outer space, to any other point on the Earth's surface. In the age of atomic bombs carried by rockets, there can be no such thing as hemisphere defence. The slaughter-house is global, and it is now all set for instant use. Is there a possibility that mankind will refrain from using it for mass-suicide? There is no possibility that we shall be able to reduce the atomic slaughter-house's scale to less than global dimensions. The progress of technology has now expanded all human operations, including genocide, to a world-wide scale. On the other hand, there is a possibility that, without changing the building's scale, we might change its use. We might be able to transform it from a global slaughter-house for the whole human race into a global home for them. This change of use would be an extreme one; but the invention of the atomic weapon has confronted mankind with this extreme choice between committing mass-suicide and learning to live together as a single family. My point is that, whether we choose life and good or whether we choose death and evil, it is certain that whatever we choose to do will have to be done on a global scale.

Is there any movement in the World today that offers us a hope that our choice may be to save ourselves from suicide by living, in future, as a single family? There is one world-wide present-day movement that does lead in this direction, and this movement is, to my mind, by far the greatest and most significant thing that is happening in the World today —something far greater and more significant than the current competition between rival ideologies and rival states which pre-occupies the attention of both the Soviet Union and the United States. There is a movement on foot for giving the benefits of civilization to that huge majority of the human race that has paid for civilization, without sharing in its benefits, during the first five thousand years of civilization's existence. This movement is a world-wide one, and Latin America is one of the regions in which it is specially in evidence. It is, I believe, the prime mover behind almost everything that is now happening in contemporary Latin America in almost every sphere of human activity. In all parts of the civilized world down to our time, extreme social injustice has been the rule. Latin America has not been peculiar in being an example of this. Latin America has, however, perhaps been slower than some other parts of the Western World—for instance, the United States, Canada, North-Western Europe, New Zealand, and Australia—to revolt against this ancient occupational disease of the so-called civilized societies. Latin America, in her turn, is revolting against social injustice now. This moral awakening is the yeast that is producing the revolutionary ferment in Latin America today. In Latin America this movement was, no doubt, overdue; for in pre-twentieth-century Latin America the degree of social injustice was rather extreme. On the other hand, there was something in the Latin American tradition that responded to this movement, and this was the sensitive Latin American feeling for the uniqueness and the dignity of human personalities.

Here, I think, we have put our finger on the source of the movement for social justice that is sweeping over the World in our time. This particular feature of the Latin American tradition is obviously a legacy from the Spanish and Portuguese tradition, and this is derived from the Christian and Muslim traditions. Christianity and Islam, like the other missionary religions, believe in the absolute value of every human being, irrespective of his or her poverty or wealth or worldly insignificance or eminence. Social justice in the form of spiritual justice has always been asserted by the Christian Church. But in the eighteenth century the demand in Western Christendom for social justice overflowed from the religious into the secular province of social life. Some of the movement's new secular manifestations were the eighteenth-century philosophy of 'the Enlightenment' in France and other continental European countries, the anti-slavery movement in Britain, and the North American, French, and Latin American revolutions against the European *ancien régime*.

If the movement for social justice had spread into the secular field at any earlier date in mankind's history, it would have been utopian. Before the nineteenth century, the human race did not possess the productive power required for distributing the benefits of civilization among more than a small privileged minority. Since the nineteenth century, we have seen a progressive increase in human productivity as a result of the application of science to technology; and it is this that has changed the vision of secular, as well as religious, social justice for all human beings from being a utopian dream into becoming a reasonable ambition. Within the last two hundred years the increase of productivity through the application of science has already gone far, but apparently this technological revolution is still in its infancy. Technology is, of course, an ethically neutral force. The enhanced power that it places in human hands can be used, at will, for either good or evil. We are aware today that we may be going to use it for committing mass-suicide. But, if we bring ourselves to use our enormous new power for creation instead of for destruction, then there is no doubt that a progressing technology will enable us eventually to give substantial social justice to the whole human race, if we choose

The word 'eventually' is a crucial one in this context.

If we refrain from committing mass-suicide, the eventual attainment of the glorious goal of universal social justice may be a certainty. But it is also certain that the road leading towards this goal is going to be a long and a rough one, and it is probable that we shall suffer many frustrations and set-backs on the way. We have suffered quite a number of these already; and, here too, Latin America's experience has been a fair sample of all mankind's. The cornucopia is now in existence; but it is not going to be easy to make it churn out abundance for everybody in all parts of the World.

Here are some of the obstacles that have to be overcome. Technology cannot be put to work unless one has the necessary number of skilled technicians and managers. These exist already in fairly adequate numbers in the regions in which the Industrial Revolution first exploded. But this is only a small part of the World. The world-wide diffusion of technological skill and managerial efficiency is going to take time. Nor is this enough, by itself, to make modern technology bear its fruit. To be fruitful, it needs, not just a handful of skilled experts, but a whole population of educated men and women. The universal diffusion of education, even elementary education, is going to take still more time; for, till recently, the great majority of mankind has been illiterate. General education is less difficult to establish in cities than it is in the countryside; and the drift of the World's population out of the countryside into the rapidly growing cities is one of the major social changes in our time. All the same, the majority of the human race is still living in the countryside, and will continue to live there for a long time to come in Latin America as well as in Asia and Africa. And, unless and until general education prevails in the countryside as well as in the cities, the productivity of the World's agricultural workers is going to remain low. They will have neither the special skill nor the general enlightenment that are required for the effective application of modern science to agricultural production. Nor will they have the equipment; for the old-fashioned peasant has always lived near the margin of bare subsistence. He does not possess the capital needed for equipping him to make the land produce its full potential harvest. If the capital is provided, it will have to come from somewhere else, whether as a loan or as a gift. And the World's stock of capital is at present inadequate. Even the affluent countries, which are a small minority, have accumulated, so far, barely enough capital to finance the extension of social justice to the whole of their own peoples, not to speak of financing this for the whole wide World.

All these difficulties that lie in the path of social justice are illustrated dramatically in the present-day situation in this or that Latin American country. Mankind's ultimate source of increase in productivity is the application of human industry to potentially fertile but hitherto inadequately utilized land. Population is increasing faster in Latin America today than in any other region. The average annual rate here is now $2\frac{1}{2}$ per cent. per annum, as contrasted with an average rate of only 1·6 per cent. in Asia. In Latin America, land shortage is also exceptional. Haiti and Santo Domingo are perhaps the only two Latin American republics in which the shortage is as acute as it is in most Asian countries. Measured by Asian standards, the shortage in Chile would count as being an ample endowment, and the existing land-reserves in the other seventeen Latin republics would be fabulous. Yet the existence of a large reserve of potentially rich agricultural land does not, of course, confer instantaneous prosperity on a country that is fortunate enough to have been endowed with this economic asset. A telling case in point is Bolivia—a country whose present

economic plight is perhaps the worst in the whole of contemporary Latin America.

Even after her ill-success in the Chaco War of 1932–5,
Bolivia still possesses tropical lowlands, east of the Andes,
which amount to about three-fifths of her present territory.
These lowlands are still almost uninhabited and unculti-
vated. They are capable of producing, in huge quantities,
those tropical crops for export that are the tropical Latin
American countries' chief source, so far, of foreign exchange. No doubt, the world price of these tropical primary
products might be depressed if a large new area were to be
suddenly brought into production. The world price of these
products anyway fluctuates, and this sometimes with disastrous effects on the economy of the producing countries. Yet,
when we have allowed for these probable deductions from
profits, the opening-up of Bolivia's virgin tropical lowlands
would still be highly profitable for her; and these particular
profits would earn for her the foreign exchange of which
she is now in desperately short supply for keeping her
economy going. She is in short supply because the former
world market for her tin has collapsed, and her reserves of
tin are also within sight of being used up.

Bolivia's one greater economic need than the production
of primary products for export is to re-establish a domestic
source of food-supply for La Paz and her other cities. This
supply used to be provided by the haciendas in Bolivia's
ancient agricultural territory on the Andean plateau. These
haciendas were not intensively or scientifically cultivated,
but they did produce a surplus of food, because they were
large-scale enterprises. The haciendas supplied the exotic
Bolivian cities at the expense of the dense Indian agricultural
population on the plateau. The standard of living of the
Indian labourers on the haciendas was painfully low; and so
was that of those Indian communities whose lands the

haciendas had not engulfed. The land shortage among the surviving Indian subsistance-farmers was acute when a handful of urban liberals made the Bolivian revolution of 1952. The new régime nationalized the tin-mines, but it had had no intention of breaking up the haciendas into fragments that would not be viable units of agricultural production. However, the Indian peasantry virtually took control of the revolution and made sweeping seizures of land and buildings. They were even able to compel the Bolivian Government to introduce into the agrarian law of 2 August 1953 an escape clause allowing the land to be divided up into lots smaller than the prescribed minimum if there should prove to be not enough land to provide holdings of that viable size for all landless rural families. There was not enough; so, in the ancient cultivated areas on the plateau, the land has been subdivided to a degree that has seriously reduced production. The food-supply for the Bolivian cities has now to come from abroad, and this new, high-priority, item in Bolivia's foreign shopping-list has worked, in combination with the loss of foreign earnings from the export of tin, to drive Bolivia into currency inflation. She has been driven into this in spite of receiving substantial and continuing economic aid from the United States.

If I am right, this United States aid has been directed, so far, mainly to those parts of the Bolivian economy that are already modern and that are consequently already in contact with the world market. It has not yet filtered down to the still depressed peasantry on the plateau; and it has not yet begun to be directed towards the opening-up of the potentially rich virgin eastern lowlands. The utilization of these is the ultimate remedy for the double economic blow that Bolivia has suffered from the collapse of her tin-mining industry and from the putting-out-of-action of the food-producing haciendas on the plateau. But the obstacles to this radical cure for Bolivia's present economic malady are formidable.

In the first place, large and expensive preliminary public works would have to be carried out. The tropical forest would have to be cleared; roads and other means of communication would have to be created in conditions of soil and climate which make the building and maintenance of roads and railways difficult and costly. Foreign capital would have to be induced to finance this, and the prospect for it would not be attractive from a business standpoint, since there could be no hope of any quick returns on the outlay. Then settlers would have to be found to populate these newly opened tropical lowland territories and to cultivate them. The desirable source for this requisite supply of man-power would be, of course, the congested Indian peasant population on the adjoining plateau. If these poor people could be transformed from being the primitive subsistence-farmers that they now are on the plateau into becoming skilled producers of cash crops in the lowlands, they would cease to be an economic liability for Bolivia and would become an economic asset for her instead. But could they be induced, even by the prospect of a rise in their standard of living, to give up their ancient habitat and habits? One of the reasons why Bolivia was worsted in the Chaco War was that her conscript soldiers from the temperate plateau could not stand the tropical climate of the lowland war-zone. Acclimatization is difficult not only physically but psychologically. It is conceivable that, when the Bolivian tropical lowlands are eventually opened up, they will be populated, not by Indians from the Bolivian plateau, but by colonists from Southern Europe: Italians, say, or Spaniards or both. In that event, Bolivia as a whole would, no doubt, benefit economically, but the present congested subsistence-farming Indian population on the plateau would continue to be the problem, for itself and for the whole country, that it is at the present time.

The history of Bolivia since 1952 illustrates both the force of the demand for social justice today and the possible awkwardness of the economic consequences of this. In Bolivia, the middle-class liberals who started the revolution have been promptly overtaken and overwhelmed by an elemental peasant revolt. In face of this, the present liberal middle-class minority régime, in co-operation with United States aid, has been trying to stabilize that section of Bolivia's economy that is oriented towards the world market. In pursuing this orthodox economic policy, 'they have frustrated some of the immediate expectations of the revolutionary groups'.[1] They have, in fact, sought to give precedence to economic efficiency over social justice; and this is perhaps characteristic of the middle-class's attitude, not only in Latin America, but everywhere. In Bolivia, however, these middle-class champions of economic efficiency have been fighting a losing battle.

In Bolivia, the demand of the masses for social justice has, so far, triumphed over the efforts of the middle class to re-establish economic efficiency. In Bolivia the middle class is weaker in numbers than it is in most other Latin American countries, while the Indians seem to have thrown up more dynamic leaders, and to have shown a greater capacity for concerted action, than they have elsewhere. At the same time, the explosive force of the demand for social justice is a phenomenon that is not peculiar to Bolivia. It has displayed itself in, for instance, Mexico and Guatemala and Cuba as well. The outcome has been different in the different cases, but the nature and the circumstances of the initial explosion have been the same in all of them. In all

[1] R. W. Patch, in Council on Foreign Relations: *Social Change in Latin America Today* (New York, 1961), pp. 157–8.

these four cases, a revolution was started by liberal middle-class elements in revolt against a previous régime that had forced the pace of the country's economic development by granting attractively favourable opportunities to foreign business enterprise. The middle-class liberal revolutionaries had intended and expected to become the masters in their national house. They were overtaken by an explosive demand from below for social justice. In Bolivia, as has been noted, the liberals have been fighting a hitherto losing battle on behalf of economic orthodoxy. In Guatemala and Cuba they put themselves at the head of the mass-revolution that they had precipitated. In Mexico they went underground, bided their time, and have succeeded latterly in taking control—so far, without provoking a violent reaction against them among the masses—after having had to let the mass-revolution run its course for thirty years.

The popular line taken by the middle-class revolutionaries in Guatemala and Cuba quickly raised a political issue that aroused such strong feelings, both locally and in the United States, that it drove both the social justice issue and the economic issue into the background. Even the facts are hotly and inconclusively disputed. There is no agreement as to the extent to which either President Arbenz or President Castro committed himself either to local Communists or to the Soviet Union. There is no agreement as to whether the overthrow of the Arbenz régime in Guatemala by counter-revolution in 1954 was, or was not, due to surreptitious United States intervention of the kind that came to light in relation to Cuba in 1961 when a United-States-aided attempt at a counter-revolution there miscarried. In Cuba the present revolution in the name of social justice is still in so early a stage that we cannot yet foresee its eventual effects on the rest of Latin America. The corresponding revolution in Guatemala has been repressed for the time being. I shall therefore leave both the Guatemalan and the Cuban revolution aside for the moment, and will concentrate on the Mexican Revolution. This is much more illuminating today, because it has already been in progress for more than half a century and has passed through a series of clearly distinguishable phases.

I will, however, note, in passing, one significant point about the history of Guatemala since the counter-revolution of 1954. The political body of the Arbenz revolution may lie amouldering in its grave, but apparently its soul goes marching on. Its soul, as I see it, is the demand for social justice, and the present counter-revolutionary régime has carried on one of the overthrown Arbenz régime's measures for doing social justice—and has done this with the aid of the North American United Fruit Company. One of the popular grievances that precipitated the Guatemalan revolution of 1944 was the United Fruit Company's holding of large reserves of land in the still undeveloped Pacific lowlands when the Guatemalan peasantry was suffering acutely from land-hunger. The United Fruit Company has since handed over a large part of its land-reserves in this region to the present counter-revolutionary régime for continuing here the colonization work that the previous revolutionary régime had initiated. This is a prudent recognition of the persisting force, in Guatemala, of the demand for social justice. It is also an attempt to give at least partial satisfaction to this demand without sacrificing economic efficiency. Guatemala's Pacific lowlands are the economic equivalent of Bolivia's eastern lowlands. They are the country's eldorado, whose eventual development might, perhaps, make it possible, in the end, to meet the demands of both economic efficiency and social justice without having to sacrifice either of these two objectives to the attainment of the other. But the point that I want, at the moment, to illustrate from the case of Guatemala is that the demand for social justice cannot be got rid of by political counter-revolution. As one of the reactionary statesmen of post-Napoleonic Europe once wittily said, 'You can do everything with bayonets except sit on them.'

In Mexico after the revolution of 1910, the first chapter in the story was the same as it has been in Bolivia since the revolution of 1952. A middle-class liberal revolutionary régime was overtaken and overwhelmed by a far more revolutionary and far more dynamic demand for social justice on the part of the peasantry and the industrial workers. The middle-class liberal revolutionaries had found themselves compelled to appeal to the masses. Without the support of these, they could not have got the upper hand over the previous masters of the country: the large landowners, the Catholic Church, the foreign investors. The liberals found that they had evoked a force that was too strong and too explosive for them to control. The Mexican middle-class liberals did not like either socialism or the re-distribution of land. Their objectives had not been these; they had been to liberate Mexico from the control of foreign capitalism and to re-establish political democracy there. But when, in 1917, the liberals sought to revive the constitution of 1857, which 'dated' in the sense that it vindicated democracy in purely political terms, the representatives of the revolutionary masses succeeded in writing large instalments of social justice into the new constitution; and they were able subsequently to put their own representatives into power in order to turn these provisions of the new constitution into achievements. Throughout the twenty years 1920–40 Mexico was under the rule of three successive presidents—Obregón, Calles, and Cárdenas—who had all risen from humble origins. Calles did much for the industrial workers; his successor Cárdenas did perhaps still more for the peasants.

Under Cárdenas's régime, there was an extensive re-distribution of the Mexican *latifundia* into peasant allotments with the juridical status of *éjidos*. Like the peasant allotments that the agrarian revolutionary Tiberius Gracchus carved out of the Italian *latifundia* in the second century B.C., the Mexican *éjidos* were not freeholds and were not alienable at the will of the peasants who held them as tenants of the national government.

The history of the Mexican revolution up to the end of Cárdenas's presidency is familiar. The characteristic note of this phase was that, throughout it, social justice was given precedence over other considerations, including that of economic efficiency. The Mexican revolution is officially a permanent one; and there is a sense in which this title is justified; for the new phase that opened with President Camacho's inauguration has been revolutionary too. Its revolutionary achievements have, however, been in another field, namely the field of economic progress. Since 1940, this, in turn, has been given precedence over other considerations, including that of social justice. The second phase of Mexico's 'Permanent Revolution' has, in fact, borne less resemblance to the first phase than it has to the preceding dictatorship of Porfirio Diaz, against which the first phase of the revolution was consciously in revolt.

The economic achievements of revolutionary Mexico since 1940 have indeed been impressive. Bolivia, Guatemala, and Cuba would be judged to have done well economically if they were to achieve, one day, even one-half or one-quarter as much as Mexico has now achieved in this field. Between 1945 and 1957, Mexico's gross national product doubled, and the output per worker increased during the same period by 35 per cent. Between 1939 and 1957, Mexican industrial output increased by 130 per cent.; and the contemporary advance in agricultural production has been no less impressive.

This more than doubled in the cash-crop-farming sector (leaving out of account the subsistence-farming sector) between 1945 and 1957. And it is noteworthy that this increase in production was in excess of the increase in the extension of the area cultivated, which was an increase of 69 per cent. only. This meant that, in the newly developed areas, agriculture was becoming more intensive. The new agriculture was on new ground, was conducted by new methods, and was allocated to cash crops. The proportion of the total cultivated area that was irrigated rose from about 28 per cent. in 1940 to about 33 per cent. in 1955. Most of the big increases in cash crops were in crops for export.

The most Diaz-like feature of this second phase of the Mexican Revolution has been the extent of the foreign participation in it and contribution to it. And, this time, the United States has been by far the greatest single participator and contributor. During these years one important source of Mexico's earnings of foreign exchange has been the annual visits of Mexican seasonal agricultural workers to the United States and of United States tourists to Mexico. The sums spent by United States tourists in Mexico have amounted to as much as about 70 per cent. of Mexican merchandise exports. In the course of the years 1945 to 1957 there was a steep rise in the amount of foreign investment in Mexico, and in 1957 nearly 80 per cent. of the total was from the United States. Between 1940 and 1957 the proportion of the United States investment in Mexico that was placed in the manufacturing industries and in commerce rose from 4.9 per cent. to 58.5 per cent.; and in the early 1950's the twenty-five largest foreign concerns in Mexico were subsidiaries of United States corporations. The first loans to the Mexican Government from private sources in the United States for thirty years were negotiated in 1948–9.

In fact, under the régime of President Camacho and his

successors, economic development has been given precedence in Mexico over nationalism as well as over social justice. And, though President Camacho's second successor President Cortinez did do something once again for the small farmer, and also sought to stem the returning tide of corruption, he did not attempt to reverse President Camacho's and President Alemán's general policy, as President Camacho had deliberately and successfully reversed President Cárdenas's.

In 1956 and 1957 nearly half the Mexican federal budget was allocated to economic development, at the expense of social welfare as well as of military expenditure. And this public expenditure has been designed, not to supplant private enterprise, but to supply it with the means of communication and with the power resources that it requires in order to expand. President Camacho promised all kinds of encouragement to industrial development, and he gave the structure of taxation a turn which favoured the accumulation of capital by industrialists, while placing burdens on consumers. He also gave precedence to the economic objective of increasing agricultural productivity over the social objective of endowing a maximum number of peasants with allotments. The Éjido Bank had been founded to promote this social purpose; but in 1954 the director of the bank is reported to have said that, while the bank did make loans to about one-third of all the *éjidarios*, its policy was to lend on the security of fertile lands, preferably on such as were irrigated, rather than to take risks over poor lands of the kind that were held and worked by most of the subsistence-farmers.[1] As a consequence of this policy, 'the great mass of the small peasant landowners . . . and about 75 per cent. . . . of the *éjidarios* are simply not reached by existing govern-

[1] U. Lewis, in Council on Foreign Relations: *Social Change in Latin America Today* (New York, 1961), pp. 318–19.

ment credit facilities and continue to be victims of local money-lenders'.[1]

As a result of government policy during the last twenty years, the great increase in Mexico's national income has been accompanied by a great inequality, and indeed inequity, in the distribution of it. The lion's share has been appropriated by the owners of capital and by the higher income groups: i.e. by the new rich and by the upper levels of the new middle class. The new rich are, no doubt, not numerous, and the new middle class has been growing rapidly in numbers at its lower levels. But this class, taken altogether, does not yet amount to more than about 20 per cent. of the whole population, and it has been estimated that 1 per cent. of the population now pockets 51 per cent. of the total national income. The poor have been growing poorer not only relatively but absolutely. In agriculture, industry, and government service, real wages are estimated to have suffered decreases of from 27 to 46 per cent. between 1939 and 1950, and the depressed classes' material conditions of life have deteriorated. Between 1940 and 1952 the population of Mexico City increased by 92 per cent.; between 1947 and 1952 the slum area increased from 3·8 per cent. to 12·7 per cent. of the city's total area. There had been a building boom since 1940, but it had been for the benefit of the upper and middle classes. In 1950, 43·2 per cent. of the population (not counting children less than six years old) was still illiterate. In the years 1950–4, only 47 per cent. of the children were at school. Post-primary education was expanding faster than primary. In 1960, more than 60 per cent. of the population was still ill-fed, ill-clothed, and ill-housed; more than 40 per cent. was still illiterate; and about 45 per cent. of the children were still not receiving any education at all.

[1] Lewis, ibid., p. 319.

This sombre social situation looks, at first sight, like a paradoxical result of a sensational aggregate increase in a nation's wealth. The infliction of this degree of social injustice looks as if it must have been wanton. Yet this repulsive picture is not, of course, a peculiarly Mexican one. To an Englishman with any knowledge of his own country's history, the picture is painfully familiar. It is the picture, not only of Mexico half-way through the twentieth century, but also of Britain round about the turn of the eighteenth and nineteenth centuries. An odious degree of social injustice persisted in Britain down to the First World War, and I myself am old enough for this to have made on me, as a child, an impression which remains vivid in my memory of it. In Britain in the course of the half century since 1914, there has been an immense social revolution in the direction of greater social justice, and happily this has been achieved without bloodshed and even without seriously embittering the former privileged classes. I hope a similar chapter of history may be in store for Mexico and also for the many other countries, in Latin America and in other regions, that have entered on the industrial revolution at later dates than my country.

But, if it is true that the movement for social justice is the characteristic and the dominant movement of our age, how does this movement come to be frustrated precisely at a time when the economic means for achieving its purposes are being created? These economic means are indispensable; without them, the vision of social justice would remain the utopian dream that it was in the days before the rise of modern technology. A great increase in economic production is not, however, something that comes by itself. Its price is hard work and austerity, and these cannot bear fruit without the application of understanding and skill. The hard work has to be done by all classes of the population alike; the no less necessary understanding and skill have been supplied, in the first phase of the industrial revolution, by a rising middle class. In this phase, this class has been master of the situation. It has been the new cornucopia's bottle-neck. So, in this phase, the middle class has taken advantage of its power to appropriate the profits for itself and to allocate the austerity to the other new class, namely the industrial workers. This is unethical. Unfortunately it is also human. Fortunately it has proved already to be a temporary phase in the history of those countries that were the first to enter on the industrial revolution. This is one reason why we can look forward with some confidence to seeing this phase pass in other countries that have entered on the same revolution at later dates.

The problem that I have just been illustrating from the current histories of four Latin American countries is obviously not confined to Latin America or to the Western Hemisphere. It is a world problem. All over the World in the past, the benefits of civilization have been monopolized by a small oligarchy of big landlords. The same benefits could not be extended to the huge depressed majority of the members of society without a revolution that had to be both political and economic. The political power of the traditional oligarchs had to be broken; the productive power of the whole community had to be raised. Both revolutions have been carried out successfully by a new class, the middle class. Without the middle class's experience and skill and initiative, this double revolution could not have been achieved, as far as one can see. The middle class's service to society was perhaps an indispensable one; and the middle class has certainly arrogated to itself a proportionate reward. It has appropriated almost the whole of the increased production which the first phase of the Industrial Revolution has generated; and, in consequence, the great majority of mankind has experienced no appreciable change for the better as a result of the middle-class revolution. From the majority's point of view, what has happened has been merely the replacement of a landlord oligarchy by a middle-class oligarchy. The hopes that the masses cherished and that the middle-class revolutionaries encouraged have been frustrated by the middle class itself as soon as it has ousted the landlords from the saddle and has taken their place.

The Mexican Revolution's volte-face since 1940 has been openly proclaimed by the Partido Revolucionario Institucional, which has been the single party in power in Mexico since 1930 without any breach of solidarity or break in continuity, in spite of the enormous change in the party's policy since the end of the last decade of the Mexican Revolution's socially revolutionary first phase. In 1950, the P.R.I. 'officially discarded the concept of the class struggle and "democracy of the workers and agrarians" in favour of the "ideal" of the "middle-classes".' [1] In June 1957 a committee of the Mexican Senate that was concerned with small rural properties reported that 'Mexico's agrarian reform . . . had been a total failure' and that 'chaos prevails in the countryside because of the present anarchy in . . . agrarian legislation'. [2]

This would be an ironical end to history. But history is not going to come to an end if mankind refrains from committing mass-suicide. Neither the movement for social justice nor the movement for the increase of economic productivity seems likely to be brought to a halt. In the first chapter of their joint history, these two movements have been in tension with each other. The promotion of social justice has been inimical to economic productivity, and conversely, the promotion of economic productivity has been

[1] J. J. Johnson : *Political Change in Latin America: The Emergence of the Middle Sectors* (Stanford, Cal., 1958, Stanford University Press), p. 149.
[2] *The New York Times*, 25 June, 1957, quoted in op. cit., p. 151.

inimical to social justice. This conflict, however, has been in the short run, at a stage in which mankind's performance has still fallen far short of achieving either objective. In the long run, on the other hand, the two movements are surely complementary.

Experience has already shown that social justice cannot make much progress without an accompanying increase in economic productivity. If this is not self-evident, it is demonstrated by the history of Mexico, Guatemala, Bolivia, and perhaps also Cuba, in our time. Perhaps it is not so immediately obvious that economic productivity cannot make much progress without an accompanying increase in social justice. Yet this, too, is surely demonstrated by the present situation in Mexico. Mankind's sole ultimate capital asset is human ability—physical, intellectual, and spiritual. This is the prime mover of the vast non-human natural forces that mankind has now harnessed. These work for us only in so far as human ability is applied to them. But human ability remains merely potential unless and until it is given the means of exerting itself; and the necessary means is well-being in the widest sense of the word. Where one half of the population still consists of poverty-stricken illiterate industrial or agricultural workers, one half of the community's potential stock of the prime economic motive force remains untapped. Economic efficiency and social justice ultimately have to go hand in hand. We cannot have much of either without having a great deal of the other as well. Our unified objective should be to drive both movements forward side by side with each other in double harness.

Of course we may fail to achieve this balance, and then the penalty will be either economic bankruptcy, such as we see in present-day Bolivia, or social injustice, such as we see in present-day Mexico. But neither of these unfortunate states of disequilibrium is likely to last for very long. The present situation in Mexico has arisen from a reaction against a situation like the present one in Bolivia. Conversely, the Mexican revolution of 1910 was a reaction against a situation like the present one in Mexico itself. A minority may succeed in monopolizing the benefits of civilization for decades or even for centuries. In the Roman Empire, the middle class managed to hold down the proletariat for about two centuries and a half. But then there came a revolutionary social explosion, and this was all the more violent for having been staved off for so long. In present-day Latin America, the eruption has been temporarily suppressed in Mexico and in Guatemala, but it has broken out with titanic force in Cuba.

In the light of past experience, it is, I think, safe to say that, whenever and wherever the middle class tries to sit on the social safety-valve, it is going to bring on itself, sooner or later, the nemesis of being blown sky high. This is a barbarous denouement, and it is also an unprofitable one for society as a whole. Society cannot afford to eliminate the middle class, because this class possesses experience and skill that is indispensable to society, and this in all fields of activity. The alternative is for the middle class voluntarily to help the industrial and agricultural labouring class to attain the middle-class standard of living. Where this policy succeeds, it creates a classless society through the amalgamation of two classes and not through the elimination of one of them: that is to say, it achieves the double objective of social justice and economic productivity by peaceful agreement, instead of missing both objectives by plunging society into a class-war.

The United States has already gone far, in its own domestic life, towards solving mankind's major present-day problem along these constructive lines, and it looks as if Western Europe may go equally far in the same direction in the near future. Of course, all human ways of life are very imperfect, and self-complacency is never warrantable. In the United States, for example, 5 or 10 per cent. of the population is still suffering social injustice; and the one thing worse than being a depressed majority is to be a depressed minority. A depressed majority does at least possess the latent strength of numbers, and, if driven to desperation, it can show its teeth and claws. A depressed minority is impotent.

A depressed minority's sole hope lies in the sensitiveness of the conscience of the affluent majority; and human consciences are apt to work sluggishly unless they have some devil to drive them. The traditional devil of Christian mythology has now ceased to be convincing, even to minds that profess still to be croyant. But, as the devil has faded out, authentic figures of flesh and blood have stepped forward, in the nick of time, to take Mephisto's place and to perform his indispensable function. Today, Karl Marx is the regional patron devil of the non-Communist World, and Fidél Castro is the regional patron devil of Latin America. As I see it, their arrival has been opportune. In my belief, we should have fared worse than we have if these public prosecutors of our Western way of life had not done us the unintended service of pricking our consciences by arousing our fears.

II

THE PRESENT REVOLUTION
IN LATIN AMERICA

TODAY I am coming to the heart of my subject—namely, the present revolution in Latin America. I will confess that I find this assignment alarming, because I am conscious that, in undertaking it, I stand convicted of audacity. It is indeed audacious for a European—and not even a Latin-speaking one, at that—to talk about Latin America to a mainly Latin American audience. My qualifications are most inadequate. I will put my cards on the table, to let you see, in advance, what they amount to.

I have visited some of the Latin American countries, but only six of them out of the twenty. Standing on the Latin American soil of Puerto Rico, I ought, perhaps, to correct my figures and say that I have now visited seven Latin American countries out of the twenty-one. After all, this Commonwealth of Puerto Rico, whose guests we are today, can measure up even to giant Brazil if we credit Puerto Rico with her continental hinterland and if we remind ourselves that this Caribbean island is now rapidly colonizing the biggest city in all North America. Still, seven countries out of twenty-one is only one-third of the whole number.

The continental Latin American countries that I have visited are Mexico, Guatemala, Panamá, Colombia, Ecuador, and Peru. My sampling has, as you see, been selective. I have managed to visit four out of the six Latin American countries that have a particularly large pre-Columbian—I mean, Indian—element in the physical composition of their present-day population. I have done this on purpose, because I already know, fairly well, two American countries—the United States and Canada—whose population is overwhelmingly trans-Atlantic in origin. By analogy with these two North American countries, I can make for myself a picture of Brazil, Uruguay, Argentina, and Chile more easily than I could have made one of the tier of 'Indian-American' countries—if I may call them that—which extends from Mexico to Paraguay inclusive, though its geographical continuity is interrupted by enclaves of European population in Costa Rica, Colombia, and Venezuela. Analogy is no substitute for direct observation. As an intellectual tool, it is notoriously treacherous. Yet it can give one at least a glimmer of understanding. So I have used my limited opportunities for direct observation in Latin America for visiting countries which I obviously could not have pictured at second hand by analogy with Canada and the United States.

There are some things in Latin American life—things that are common, I believe, to all the Latin American countries—which I can appreciate by analogy with my own national and social background. One of the features of the present Latin American revolution is, if I am right, the enduring influence, for good or evil, of the pre-revolutionary structure of Latin American society. This traditional way of life is obviously in process of dissolution. At the same time it is also obviously an active ingredient in the mixed yeast that is creating the present ferment. Consider the evolution of the Latin American middle class, which appears to me—subject to correction—to be the key social class in Latin America today. The germ of this class was the tiny band of classically educated intellectuals—lawyers, doctors, men of letters—who were its sole representatives in the colonial era. Today this academic nucleus of the Latin American middle class has been reinforced by a horde of middle-class people of a new type—people who are earning their livings, not in the so-called 'liberal professions', but in commerce and industry. The old-fashioned nucleus has been swamped by these new recruits, yet the antique middle class's tradition, though now diluted, is still, I believe, an appreciable factor in the outlook of the larger, less highly cultivated, but perhaps more practical-minded Latin American middle class of today. Well, I can enter into this Latin American story, to some extent, in the light of my own personal history. I happen to have been born into the corresponding antique nucleus of the English middle class. My education, too, was exclusively classical, and in my life-time I have seen, in England, this classical culture dissolve yet still continue to influence the semi-alien commercial and industrial middle class by which I now find myself surrounded at home. 'Semi-alien' is the right word. On my father's side, I have no ancestor who ever made his living in commerce or industry, and I have no descendants, so far, who have entered these modern fields of middle-class activity. So the history of the Latin American middle class is not a completely closed book for me.

And then I have a third spot-light on modern Latin America which may surprise you. Thanks to my classical education, I am fairly familiar with Roman history; and, when I set myself to study the structure of Latin American society and its modern evolution, I am constantly coming across features—and important features—that have a meaning for me because I know them already in their ancient Italian context.

Two outstanding features of traditional Latin American life are the social and psychological solidarity of the family in its widest extension and the patron-client relation, in which an ethical bond, comparable in emotional quality to the bond of kinship, is incongruously combined with elements of rather crass economic exploitation and social injustice. As I see it, these institutions stemming from a socially static past are still making their effect in the fluid Latin American society of today. They partially survive in camouflaged forms; and, in so far as they do not survive, they have left behind them a psychological vacuum that is one of the causes of the perceptible present-day malaise among the uprooted workers on modern Latin America's cash-crop plantations and in her mushroom-mammoth cities, if I may venture to coin this double epithet. The patron-client relation: well, that runs all through Roman history; the superfamily: well, that is the Roman 'gens'. So here I find myself on ground that I have explored before.

And then there is the Latin American oligarchy of *latifundarios*—a dominant minority which is surely doomed, yet which is dying hard and is refusing to die without first setting an imprint on the commercial and industrial 'new rich'. In the former domain of the Spanish Empire of the Indies, these Creole agrarian magnates stepped into the deposed royal government's shoes and held their ground for more than a century after the continental successor-states of the Spanish Empire had won their independence. The war of independence was launched by the academic intellectuals in the name of the exotic ideas of the North American and French revolutions. The intellectuals were allowed to write the constitutions of the new republics in this foreign idiom; but it was the *latifundarios* who took the power; and, if and when the middle-class intellectuals jibbed, the newly installed oligarchs did not hesitate to bring them to heel by wielding the whip of military dictatorship. The frustrated representatives of the liberal professions were powerless to return to the attack until they had been reinforced by new-fangled social formations which were almost as alien to them culturally as they were to the oligarchs. If the oligarchs are now fighting their last rearguard actions in a losing battle, this is due to a joint offensive of the traditional intellectuals, the new commercial and industrial wing of the middle class, and the new class of industrial workers. These new elements have partly sprung from the soil and partly arrived from overseas. Mestizos and European immigrants are their two main ingredients. And the stream of domestic migration, as well as the stream of immigration from overseas, has been flowing into the rapidly growing Latin American cities.

The oligarchy's traditional monopoly of power cannot be wrenched out of its hands unless its economic basis is cut away from under its feet. This is why the break-up of the *latifundia*, the dismantling of the *haciendas*, has been such a central issue, and such a controversial one, in the modern chapter of Latin American history. In Latin America, agrarian reform is the necessary starting-point for political, economic, and social change alike. On this point, I will quote a North American authority.

'Units of production are either too large or too small; ownership and occupancy are often precarious; the communities are tradition-bound and inflexible; farm labour conditions are not many steps removed from serfdom; land as a resource does not freely exchange hands but is hoarded and unavailable to the small cultivator. There is no "tenure ladder" in the sense that a landless person could gradually work his way into the ownership class. Owners and non-owners of land are frequently separated by strict racial and cultural class-barriers. The system reinforces the *status quo* and confers power upon those with inherited position and wealth. Farm investment is low, demand for consumer goods restricted, and large segments of the population are held at the margin of the economic mainstream in the countries. Political democracy and social mobility are greatly circumscribed.'[1]

The untoward economic and social effects of the *latifundia* do, indeed, make themselves felt far beyond their own vast expanses. The dead hand of the *latifundia* lies heavily on almost every Latin American country.

'The *minifundio-latifundio* patterns are not independent, but are often closely interrelated. Large estates are surrounded by many small *ranchos, chacras, huertas, hijuelas* or *sitios*, drawing seasonal labour from them and in many ways contributing to the maintenance of the system. The *latifundios* exercise an influence far beyond their own boundaries, and they are frequently a limiting force on regional development.'[2]

For instance, their economic autarky at a low level of economic activity prevents the provincial towns from developing commercially. It is also a drag on the development of plantations producing cash-crops for export, and on the development of urban industry.

This is why a break-up of the *latifundia* is a necessary first step for any Latin American country if it is to get on the move economically and socially. But this indispensable revolutionary act raises some highly debatable questions. Is the break-up of the *latifundia* a positive end in itself? Or is it merely one of several alternative possible means of doing social justice to landless peasants by providing allotments for them? Might it not be better to provide for this by opening

[1] T. F. Carroll: 'The Land Reform Issue in Latin America', in A. O. Hirschman [ed.]: *Latin American Issues* (New York, 1961, The Twentieth Century Fund), p. 176.
[2] Carroll, ibid., p. 167.

up and colonizing the rich virgin lands of which there is still an abundance? No doubt this would be a slower process, as well as a more costly one. But it would minimize the risk of agrarian reform producing a political explosion, and it would serve the national interest by bringing into productivity a potential national asset which the country cannot afford to leave unutilized. The arguments for evading a break-up of the *latifundia* are specious, and the political power of the *latifundiarios'* vested interest is great. Moreover, the issue is complicated and confused by the fact that some *latifundia* have been converted into efficient modern plantations producing cash-crops, and that some of the entrepreneurs who have made this agrarian economic revolution have been, not the hereditary owners of the converted estates, but foreign purchasers of them. The area covered by these economically up-to-date plantations may be small compared with the area of the *latifundia* that are still being cultivated in the old way, at low tension. But the new plantations are important economically out of proportion to their area, because they are the main source of the foreign exchange required for financing imports—and these imports include capital goods needed for industrial development as well as the luxury consumer goods imported by a tiny rich minority.

The resistance to the redistribution of the *latifundia* has, so far, been astonishingly and distressingly successful. In 1961 it was estimated that, in Latin America as a whole and on the average, 90 per cent. of the land still belonged to only 10 per cent. of the landowners. If this estimate is even approximately correct, the concentration of land-ownership in Latin America is markedly greater than it is in any other region of comparable size. In Latin America in 1961, farms running to not more than 20 hectares in area are reckoned to have amounted to 72·6 per cent. of the total number of farms, but to have occupied only 3·7 per cent. of the total land area. On the other hand, farms running to 1,000 hectares and upwards are reckoned to have occupied 64·9 per cent. of the total land area, but to have amounted to only 1·5 per cent. of the total number of farms.

Striking examples of the still prevalent concentration of land-ownership are offered by a number of Latin American countries which resemble each other in this point of capital importance, however much they may differ from each other in other respects.

'In Guatemala, 516 farms (0·15% of all farms) represent 41% of the agricultural land. In Ecuador, 705 units (0·17%) include 37% of the farm land. In Venezuela, 74% of the farm acreage, comprising 6,800 units (1·69% of all farms), is in holdings of over 1,000 hectares. Half the farm land in Brazil is in the hands of 1·6% of the owners. In Nicaragua, 362 owners have control over fully one-third of the agricultural acreage. The most extreme concentration could be observed in Bolivia prior to the land reform. There 92% of the land was in fewer than 5,500 units, representing 6·4% of all farms.' [1]

The Mexican and Cuban pictures are similar, and these two cases are particularly significant.

In Mexico, the redistribution of the land was the first item on the agenda of the Permanent Revolution for the first thirty years of its course, and, during the last six years of these thirty, when President Cárdenas was in office, re-distribution was in fact carried out whole-heartedly by a disinterested statesman wielding the Presidency's enormous powers. Yet Cárdenas failed to break the back of the Mexican agrarian problem. His failure is declared in the follow-

[1] Carroll, ibid., p. 163.

ing figures relating to the year 1950. In that year, 42·2 per cent. of Mexican workers on the land were still landless, as against only 29·2 per cent. who were *éjidarios* and a further 26·5 per cent. who were owner-operators. Less than 1 per cent. of all farms in private hands occupied 76 per cent. of the total farm land in private hands.

As for Cuba, her land-reform law of May 1959 is important in virtue of being one of those acts of the present Cuban revolution that have set a standard—and a pace—for reform in the rest of Latin America. The pre-revolutionary land situation was in the same crying need for reform in Cuba as it was and still is in many other Latin American countries. In Cuba in 1946, 69·6 per cent. of the farms ran to not more than 25 hectares in area and occupied not more than 11·2 per cent. of the total area under cultivation. On the other hand, the farms running to 1,000 hectares and upwards occupied 36·1 per cent. of the total area under cultivation, though they amounted to no more than 5 per cent. of the total number of farms. In Cuba at the outbreak of the revolution, only about one-half of the potential farm land was under cultivation. There was chronic underemployment of agricultural labour, and at the same time there were huge imports of food from abroad.

About three-quarters of the cultivable area in pre-revolutionary Cuba was controlled by the sugar plantations. And here Cuba, which was socially so backward, was economically in the vanguard of the Latin American world. A high proportion of Cuba's large estates had been converted from self-sufficient *haciendas*, working at low tension, into efficient plantations, producing a cash-crop for export. It is noteworthy that, so far, the Cuban revolution has not followed suit to the Mexican and Bolivian revolutions or to the abortive Guatemalan revolution in its agrarian policy. It seems to be making a more constructive attempt to combine the doing of social justice to the agricultural population with the maintenance of agricultural productivity. The revolutionary Cuban Instituto Nacional de Reforma Agraria has been quick to expropriate the *latifundia* but slower in redistributing them; and the law of May 1959 contains provisions for efficient farming and for the organization of co-operatives. In 1959–60, agricultural production in Cuba did not decline. So far, the Cuban story has not been following the course of the Bolivian one.

Perhaps it does need a revolutionary explosion of fifty-megaton power to blow up the agrarian road-block that has hitherto obstructed both economic and social progress in Latin America so grievously. The landlords have been successful in resisting, not only adequate land-redistribution, but also adequate land-taxation. And their utilization of the vast areas of land under their control shows a poor performance. The cash-crop plantations, which do make efficient use of the lands that they cultivate, are also apt to hold large areas of cultivable land in reserve. Cuba is not the only example of this. In Guatemala, for instance, farmers with holdings of 1,000 hectares and upwards were cultivating, in 1950, only 5 per cent. of their holdings on the average, so it is said.

For these reasons, a frontal attack on the *latifundia* would surely have to be made for the sake of economic efficiency and fiscal equity, even if all the landless agricultural workers and all the owners of economically non-viable *minifundia* could be provided for by the opening up of potentially rich virgin lands. However, the North American authority whom I am here following points out that colonization schemes have not amounted to much so far, and, in his opinion, they are not going to solve Latin America's agrarian problem.

'In terms of potential production increases, the already established areas offer a much greater, more immediate, and less expensive possibility'[1]—

always supposing that, where new small holders are installed, they are not simply planted on an allotment and then left to their own resources, but are provided with the equipment for farming their land efficiently.

Well, in painting you this picture of Latin America's present agrarian problem, I could almost as well have borrowed my colours from a different source. Instead of drawing, as I have done, on a contemporary North American member of the staff of the United Nations Food and Agriculture Organization in present-day Rome, I could have cited some Ancient Roman historian; for, here again, Roman history has anticipated the modern Latin American story. At Rome, too, an agrarian oligarchy stepped into a deposed monarchy's shoes. At Rome, too, the oligarchy was eventually deposed, in its turn, by the combined efforts of new commercial and industrial elements: the new rich, a new middle class, a new urban proletariat. The city of Rome, too, like the cities of present-day Latin America, was swollen up to mammoth size by a double stream of migration. In Rome's case, one stream came from the Italian countryside, and the other from the Levant, which was Roman Italy's Europe. In Roman history, too, the oligarchy died far harder than the ancient monarchy. The revolution precipitated by Tiberius Gracchus's agrarian reforms thundered on, crescendo, for a hundred years and shook the Mediterranean World to pieces before Augustus succeeded, at last, in bringing it under control.

Now that I have opened my bag and shown you my tools, I must try to get on with my job. Since I am conscious that

[1] Carroll, ibid., p. 197. Cp. p. 200.

I am speaking in a company whose other members know much more about our subject than I do, I am going to try to make this contribution of mine raise a series of questions. This method will, I hope, answer to the plan of operations that the University and the Weatherhead Foundation have laid down for us. The purpose for which they have asked me to give these lectures is to lead on to a discussion. My first questions will be concerned with the changing structure of society, my later ones with some of those unstable factors in the Latin American economy that are pregnant with possibilities of political and social upheaval.

Since Latin America is divided today into twenty or (counting Puerto Rico) twenty-one separate political units, I had better begin by raising the question whether Latin America has any unity to counterbalance her diversity. The diversity is obvious, and it goes far deeper than the political level. I have already touched on the distinction between countries in which the physical composition of the population is mainly pre-Columbian and countries in which it is mainly European. In Latin America, happily, this racial distinction is not important, and this is very much to Latin America's credit. The traditional structure of Latin American society has, of course, been hierarchic; but the classes have never hardened into closed castes, and the present tendency is for them to become increasingly fluid.

Take the case of the Indian communities in the 'Indian-American' countries. Socially and culturally, no doubt, these communities are still alien worlds that have not been incorporated into the national life of the countries in whose territories they live—and had already been living for thousands of years before the Spanish conquest. But, if I am right, any individual Indian man or woman in, say, Peru can easily 'pass' (to use the North American word) from the Indian world into the modern world. To achieve this, he or she has only to fulfil three requirements. One must learn to speak Spanish, one must take to wearing modern dress, and one must migrate from one's Indian village community to a city or, short of that, to a plantation producing a cash-crop. On these terms, an ex-Indian, if he rises in the world by luck or merit, can end up as President of the Republic and as the husband of the daughter of one of the traditional oligarchs. Every opportunity is open to him, once inside, and the terms of entry are not exacting. Why, on these terms, every citizen of the United States who has African blood in his veins would have 'passed' long ago; and Latin Americans of African race have, I believe, all been assimilated in fact. The Indians have not all been assimilated yet; and, so long as they stay in their own villages, they remain insulated from the national life. All the same, the process of assimilation, through the easy 'passing' of individuals, has already gone very far. In Mexico, as well as in Peru, a great majority of the present-day population consists of *Ladinos*: that is to say, Spanish-speaking people leading a modern way of life who are *mestizos* or pure Indians in race; and in both countries the *mestizos* are numerically predominant over their fellow countrymen of pure Indian race, including Indians who have been Latinized already as well as those who have not been Latinized yet.

The civilized Indian peoples have their own diverse histories and cultures, and, in being decanted into the Latin society of, say, Mexico or Guatemala or Peru, they have, no doubt, brought with them a tincture of their own cultural past. I have had glimpses of some of these Indian communities: the Indians of Tehuántepec, whose features and dress might lead one to mistake them for veritable Indians from Asia; the Maya in Yucatan and in Northern Guatemala; the Chamulas on the Las Casas plateau; the Quechua-speaking Indians round Cuzco. Their diversity hits the traveller in the eye. Present-day Mexican intellectuals with European blood in their veins are almost aggressively conscious of Mexico's distinctive pre-Columbian cultural heritage. Cauhtémoc is their hero; Cortés is their villain. In Mexico, I am told, statues of Cortés are banned (and, now that I come to think of it, I cannot remember ever having seen a statue of William the Conqueror in England). The art of pre-Columbian Middle America is the inspiration of the potent Mexican art of our time. In the European-American republics, the different strains of European immigrant may have had a similar differentiating effect. Anyway, each Latin American nation has been steadily developing its own distinctive national characteristics. Presumably this would have happened even if the whole population of Latin America had been racially homogeneous. Experience counts for more than race in the development of ways of life, and the Latin American countries—and also the regions of which each of them is composed—have been living more or less separate lives since the beginning of history.

They have been kept separate by the inadequacy of their means of communication. Their isolation from each other has now at last been overcome by the advent of the air age. Yet, even today, only 10 per cent. of the Latin American countries' aggregate foreign trade is with each other. South America, like Australia and unlike North America, is a continent whose population is concentrated in a belt round the coasts. Till lately, at any rate, many Latin American cities were in closer communication with New York, London, Liverpool, Hamburg, or Bremen than they were with other cities in their own country, not to speak of other countries of the Latin American World. They are still relatively isolated from each other, if we take as our standard the close-meshed network of communications in the present-day world as a whole.

This continuing isolation is a serious hindrance to economic progress, and particularly to the growth of Latin American industry. Even if we leave out of account the diminutive Latin American republics in Central America and in the Antilles, the average scale of a Latin American country's economic structure is too small to provide a home market for an indigenous industry that is struggling to be born. There are, of course, exceptions. Brazil is a giant; Mexico is an economic athlete; and Brazil, as well as Mexico, is attracting North American investment. Most Latin American countries, however, would improve the prospects for their nascent indigenous industries considerably if they could manage to club together with some of their neighbours to provide a common market for the industries of each and all of the partners. Attempts along these lines are being made, as we know. We also know how slowly and hesitantly these attempts are progressing. It is at least an auspicious new factor in the situation that North American support for economic integration in Latin America has been promised by President Kennedy in his White House address of 13 March 1961, in which he launched his plan for an 'Alliance for Progress'.

The mutual isolation and the diversity of the Latin American countries are conspicuous. All the same, these countries have at least two experiences in common, and both these experiences have an important bearing on Latin America's future.

Eighteen of the twenty countries—or nineteen of the twenty-one, counting in Puerto Rico—are successor-states of the Spanish Empire of the Indies, and they have all inherited from their mother-country a common language and a common background of habits, ideas, and ideals. After making a round-trip of Spanish-America and duly noting the present-day differences between these nineteen states, a contemporary observer would do well to pay a visit to the Archives of the Indies at Seville in Andalusía. This marvellous collection of documents serves the student as a lens through which he can peer backwards into the past. As he peers, he finds that the nineteen lines, which splay so far apart on the present-day horizon, converge, as he pursues them back, until, at vanishing point, they unite. Giant Brazil, of course, is not in this Spanish company; yet Brazil's European mother-country shares with the nineteeen Spanish-American countries' European mother-country an immense common past. Spain and Portugal have in common the cultural backgrounds of the Caliphate of Córdoba and of the Roman Empire before that.

The Latin American countries' second common experience is still more important. This experience is not a legacy from the past; it is a living present-day reality. It is also an experience that all the Latin American countries share, not only with each other, but with the greater part of the contemporary world. The Latin American countries are marching in that long, and ever lengthening, procession of so-called under-developed countries that are striving to catch up with North America and North-Western Europe in mankind's social and economic advance. All countries in this procession are engaged on a forced march over broken ground. This is a heart-breaking, as well as a back-breaking, experience. An English observer can enter into it imaginatively, and also, I hope, sympathetically, because it is the experience that Britain went through at the turn of the eighteenth and nineteenth centuries, when she was blazing the trail for an industrial revolution which has now become almost world-wide. These common efforts and sufferings make a bond that is stronger than ideological differences. Some of the so-called under-developed peoples are committed ideologically to Communism, others to freedom of private enterprise; a majority are uncommitted; and I suspect that quite a number of the countries that are committed officially are uncommitted at heart. This almost world-wide framework is the one within which we have to view the present revolution in Latin America if we are to see it in its true lineaments and proportions. The dominant features in this revolutionary landscape are common to the whole of Latin America because they are common to the greater part of the World.

The landscape has one general characteristic, on which its particular characteristics are so many variations. Latin America, like the rest of the 'under-developed' three-quarters of the World, has moved out of a static traditional way of life, in which change was the exception, into a dynamic way of life, in which change is the rule. The traditional way of life was on a low economic and social level; but it gave its victims certainty. They knew what was in store for them, for good or for evil. The revolutionary way of life is carrying its victims away, at an accelerating pace, into an inscrutable future. The lure is the recognition of the possibility of a better life, and the hope of attaining it; the risk is the possibility of a miscarriage which would make the *ancien régime* look, by comparison, like a golden age in retrospect. The spirit of the *ancien régime* was melancholia tempered by resignation. The spirit of the revolution is anxiety animated by hope and at the same time exasperated by disappointment. In living in this latter atmosphere, which is such a dramatic change from the past, contemporary Latin America is a typical child of its age. The people of a developing country have to contend simultaneously with three major disturbances of the traditional tenor of life. They have to contend with deracination, with urbanization, and with economic frustration. Long-deferred and hard-won improvements in the economic lot of a struggling class may be more than cancelled by a sudden attack of inflation that makes their last state worse than their first. A national effort to increase the production of a commodity that will earn foreign exchange on the world market may be stultified by fluctuations in the world price due to an increase of production at home or elsewhere or to a decline in the demand abroad.

In the old world of the village community and the *hacienda*, the peasant, living materially perhaps not far above the starvation line, had the psychological relief of finding himself in a hierarchical society in which he was sure of his place. He was a member of his widely ramifying family; he was the client of his patron; and he was a son of the Church, which, as he knew it, was represented by his parish priest.

I have sat in one of those profusely decorated baroque village churches in the Puebla district of the Mexican plateau and have watched the villagers tending it. I say 'tending' because it was evident that, for them, their church was not an inanimate construction of stone and wood and plaster, but was a beloved living creature—a member of the family, like the children and the domestic animals. One villager was touching up the gilding on a plaster cherub's head; another was polishing the brass-work; others were practising peals on the bells. Their church was the centre of their community life and was a satisfying focus for their affections. Manifestly this was a life that made for happiness.

In another Mexican village on Labour Day, I found myself between two worlds. Out of doors in the plaza the men were celebrating this secular fiesta by holding a public meeting to the cheerful accompaniment of the village band. But inside the church the women and children were going the round of the saints, paying their respects to each venerated plaster figure in turn. This church had a particularly beautiful interior; and I think the women were getting more happiness than the men were out of their way of spending their common holiday.

Modernization means migration from the village or the *hacienda* to the plantation or to the city; and migration cuts the peasant's roots. He necessarily loses his rural patron, and he is likely to lose the Church as well. When, about two hundred years ago, the Western movement for social justice began to overflow from religious life into secular life, neither the Catholic Church nor any of the other established churches of Western Christendom kept pace with this expansion of the field of a movement which had started within the Church's bosom. They stayed within their customary ecclesiastical bounds and left the cause of secular social justice to be championed by laymen who were indifferent to religion if not positively hostile to it for what seemed to them like a callous betrayal of its mission. This breach between established religion and the campaign for secular social justice has been a tragedy for the Western World, and therefore for the World as a whole, since, in the modern age, the Western minority of mankind has been leading the non-Western majority by the nose. The breach between religion and secular social idealism has now made its appearance all over the World, and today this breach is a wide one. Sincere endeavours to bridge it have been made from both sides, but the gulf remains unclosed.

In these unhappy circumstances the peasant who migrates to the city is likely to lose most of his customary psychological and spiritual supports without having been able to wean himself from feeling the need for them. A President Cárdenas is, no doubt, a more disinterested and benevolent 'protector of the poor' than the local *hacendado* whom the revolutionary President has justly evicted. But the *hacendado* was accessible, whereas the President is remote. The peasant engulfed in the city may find the political party or the trade union less remote than the President; these new secular organizations may prove, in fact, to be as demanding as the Church used to be. But these relatively prosaic institutions can hardly fill the place that the Church used to occupy in the peasant's imagination and affection. In his urban exile —and it is exile, even if it has been voluntary—the peasant is being offered a stone in place of bread. His psychological plight is a painful one.

The material setting of this tragedy is urbanization, and this drift of population into the cities is now taking place everywhere. In a seventeen months' journey round the World in the years 1956 and 1957, I saw the same spectacle in Peru, Australia, Indonesia, India, Pakistan, Persia, 'Iraq. Every other aspect of life might be different in different regions, but this aspect was monotonously and dismally uniform. I felt it most poignantly of all in the Peruvian highland oasis of Arequipa.

Arequipa is one of the loveliest places that I have yet set eyes on anywhere in the World. No doubt it is well known to other members of this conference besides me. The sparkle in the air; the blueness of the sky; the whiteness of the snow on the symmetrical row of three huge yet graceful volcanoes; the greenness of the irrigated land by contrast with the sudden drabness of the rock at the line where the water stops: all this is ravishing till one turns a corner and catches sight of one of the shanty-towns that are now besieging the mellow city. The economic capacity of Arequipa is rigidly limited by the physical limits imposed on irrigation by the lie of the land. Every square foot than can be irrigated and cultivated has been utilized long since. And a limited agricultural area can support only a limited amount of urban trade and commerce. Arequipa offers no vacant economic opportunities, yet Indians from the higher highlands to the east are abandoning their ancestral *minifundia* to live in

squalor in Arequipa's new suburban slums without any prospect of finding any remunerative employment there. The
civic authorities try to explain the situation, and they beg the
squatters to return to their ancestral homes; but these
rational counsels fall on deaf ears. The whisper has gone
round the World that an eldorado is to be found if one will
just make the effort to get up and go to seek it; and, for the
peasantry of the south-east Peruvian highlands, eldorado
means Arequipa. At Baghdad, next year, I found myself
looking at just such another shanty-town swarming with
just such another horde of pathetically expectant peasant
squatters.

The biggest Latin American city that I have seen so far
is Mexico City. I have still to see colossal Buenos Aires and
gigantic São Paulo and Rio. The four Latin American cities
that I have just mentioned would rank as large cities even if
they were transplanted to the most highly urbanized regions
of North America or Europe. But absolute size is not the
most revealing gauge of a city's potency. What counts is the
degree to which a city dominates the country on which it has
been spawned; and, on this test, a smaller city in a smaller
country—for instance, Montevidéo in Uruguay—may be a
more illuminating sample of urbanization.

In North America and North-Western Europe and Australia today, the cities are draining the countryside almost
dry of population. Urban industry is equipping the land
with mechanical apparatus that enables an ever smaller
number of hands to produce an ever larger yield per acre.
The agricultural labour that is thus being rendered superfluous migrates to the city, and the labour that remains on
the land becomes a kind of *urbs in rure* : a population that
is urban in habits and in outlook, though its industrial job
happens to be that of food-production. Australia is perhaps
the country in which this process of urbanization in both the

literal and the cultural sense has gone the farthest up to date. A rural population may also be urbanized in a country where, in spite of industrialization, the rural population remains thick on the ground simply because the cities have already been filled to saturation point. An example of this is Japan. In most Latin American countries too, the agricultural section of the population continues to account for a high percentage of the total, though the cities here are growing as fast as anywhere in the World and the urban section's percentage is gradually rising. In Latin America, however, in contrast to North America, North-Western Europe, Australia, and Japan, the rural population is not yet being permeated by the urban way of life; and there is here a social and cultural gulf between the city and the countryside, in spite of the fact that a high proportion of the population of the cities consists of uprooted peasants.

The cities of Spanish America have, of course, always been exotic since the time of their foundation during and after the Spanish conquest. Like the Greek cities planted in Egypt and South-West Asia by Alexander the Great and his successors, the Spanish-American cities have been foreign plums insinuated into a native cake. This sowing of alien cities creates a severe internal tension in a country that has been subjected to the treatment. It accentuates the ecological contrast between town and country by super-imposing a cultural contrast upon it. For about three hundred and fifty years, running from the early decades after the Spanish conquest to the closing decades of the nineteenth century, Spanish America was an almost unique example of the reappearance of this Hellenistic phenomenon in the modern world. But today the exotic modern city has become ubiquitous. Mexico City and Guayaquil and Lima have Asian counterparts in Ankara, Tehran, Kabul, Karachi, Bombay, Djakarta. And these new-fangled cities are much more akin to each other than each of them is to the countryside in which it is marooned.

Do you happen to possess a magic carpet that can transport whole cities, as single frame-houses are transplanted every day in Princeton, New Jersey? If you do possess one (and there is no mechanical gadget that is incredible nowadays), I suggest that you try a sociological experiment. Pluck up two of these standardized exotic cities—say Lima and Tehran—in the small hours and transpose their positions. I will wager that when the Persian peasant turns up next morning for market in Lima, and the Peruvian peasant in Tehran, he will suffer no shock, because he will not be aware of any change. The cities of the present-day world, which are so exotic in their respective rural settings, are as like each other as so many specimens of some standardized part of a mass-produced automobile. Substitute one specimen for another; the engine will run as efficiently as before, and the rustic driver will not find the machine any more fantastic now than he found it previously.

All over Latin America and all over the World, the uprooted peasantry is now pouring into these standardized exotic cities, and is being subjected to the revolutionary ordeal of an abrupt change-over from a static rural way of life to a fluid urban one. And then, as if this one ordeal were not enough, the still peasant-minded newcomer to the city has to acclimatize himself there under the buffets of a neverceasing blizzard of inflation. The cause of this economic malady is not obscure. The hitherto under-developed countries are pressing forward with their belated development at a pace, and on a scale, that are perpetually outrunning their flagging economic resources. A remedy—at any rate a lasting remedy—is not so easy to devise and apply. Meanwhile, the social and psychological effects are distressing and alarming.

Inflation is an engine of social injustice by its very nature.

It robs those classes that are condemned to live on fixed incomes for the benefit of those that are not, and this inevitably creates social tension by making the victims feel that they are being cheated—as indeed they are. Inflation is therefore a fertile mother of revolt and revolution always and everywhere. But its exasperating effect is doubly strong where, as in present-day Latin America, the classes that it hits are newcomers who have made great sacrifices in the hope of realizing proportionately great expectations. In present-day Latin America, this is the situation of the callow industrial working class and the hardly less callow lower strata of the middle class's new industrial and commercial and public service wing. These new recruits to the middle class are salaried employees, and inflation victimizes them, as it victimizes the industrial workers, to the profit of the upper middle class and of the new rich, who are masters of an inflationary situation because they are the owners of the means of industrial production and of commercial exchange.

If inflation in Latin America is going to be hard to cure, the problem presented by the fluctuation in the world prices of Latin America's primary products is going to be perhaps even harder to deal with. For as far as one can see ahead, the Latin American countries are going to depend on the sale abroad of these primary products for the maintenance and development of their economies. These cannot be developed, or even maintained, without the continuing purchase abroad of elaborate capital equipment which no Latin American country is yet within sight of being able to produce for itself at home in sufficient quantities up to a high enough quality at an economic price. This is, no doubt, the most serious of all the Latin American problems which Latin Americans will expect the United States to face, and, if possible, solve, in co-operation with them. It is an economic problem on the surface, but is a social and political one in its volcanic depths. It is significant and encouraging that President Kennedy has grasped this nettle—and it is a stinging one from the North American standpoint—in his White House address of 13 March 1961, in which he launched his plan for an 'Alliance for Progress'.

I will close this lecture by summarizing the gist of it in the words of an authoritative North American observer.

'Latin America is in the process of upheaval. It is one of the most dramatic and explosive movements in all history. An industrial revolution, urbanization, the growth of a middle class, a population explosion unequalled anywhere in the World, a political ferment that is introducing all the revolutionary doctrines of democracy, a social revolution in which the masses who accepted ignorance, poverty, and disease as the natural course of events are now demanding and beginning to get equality of opportunity, education, health, and a higher standard of living—all these and other dynamic forces are creating a situation comparable in its way, and in the impact it is going to have on the Western World, to the European Renaissance.'[1]

[1] Herbert L. Matthews, in *The United States and Latin America* (New York, 1959, The American Assembly of Columbia University), p. 188.

III

THE PROBLEM FOR THE
UNITED STATES

I ONCE saw a very big dog blunder into a strange house. This huge creature had a warm heart. For him, every human being, known or unknown, whom he met was, *ex officio*, a friend. So, when he found himself in a room full of people, his heart glowed; and, since his psychosomatic gearing was perfect, his feelings immediately expressed themselves in the appropriate physical actions. It was then that the trouble began; for the actions that were appropriate to the dog's feelings were not appropriate to the room which he had entered uninvited. The first swinge of his tail broke a chair leg. The second swinge overturned a dumb waiter, with a crash of breaking china and a cascade of ruined crackers and cookies on to the floor. The third swinge sent a cushion hurtling against the incandescent wires of an electric heater, where the cushion stuck and caught fire. By this time the room was in an uproar, and the innocent cause of this was being cursed, kicked, and cuffed by the indignant human inmates. The poor dog did not notice the havoc that he had made, but he did notice the hostility with which he was being treated, and I shall never forget the piteous bewildered look in his eyes as he made his rueful exit. 'These humans', his eyes said, 'are incomprehensible. I demonstrate my affection for them, and they treat me as if I had committed an offence.'

The dog could not understand that his offence was the incorrigible one of just being a dog of his size. Had he been a lapdog, he could have demonstrated his affection with impunity. The trouble was that he was a great dane, and it was difficult to see what he could do about this built-in handicap to good relations; for it is just as impossible to subtract a cubit from one's stature as it is to add one to it.

My first visit to the United States was in 1925. I was at a summer-school on international relations at Williams College, Williamstown, Massachusetts. One of the round tables was on relations between the United States and Latin America, and one of the experts who addressed us was the then President of the United Fruit Company, Mr Lee Cutter. The subject of his talk was 'tact', and he illustrated his points by anecdotes which were, I am sure, all true stories, taken straight out of his corporation's annals. It was not tactful, Mr Cutter said, to place one's local branch office in a Central American republic's capital city. The building would overshadow the dome of the Capitol, and that would not be tactful, he said. It was not tactful either, if one's company owned and ran the only railroad in the republic, and if the president of the republic had asked for and been granted a special train, for one's local branch manager to side-track the president's special train while the branch manager's own special train went ahead. This, too, was not tactful, said Mr Cutter.

Years passed before I was able to appreciate the wisdom of the first of Mr Cutter's rules of tact by observing a case in which this rule had been disregarded—not by Mr Cutter's company, but by another North American concern of the same calibre. Visit the principal cities along the Pacific coast of Central and South America; you will find them dominated by the local branch offices of the Grace Line, and you will probably agree with Mr Cutter that this is not tactful. But, of course, it is easier to convict the Grace Line of tactlessness than to tell them how they can avoid it. Being, as I suppose it is, the most important single business concern, foreign or national, in each of these Pacific-coast Latin American countries, the Grace Line has to locate its branch offices in some central and accessible position. And the company has to provide itself with as many cubic feet of office space as the volume of its business requires. One is bound to grant this, and, when one has granted it, the damage to public relations has already been done. The local Grace Line building has soared into the stratosphere, dwarfing the national capital's puny public buildings down there below. Being a giant may be good for one's balance sheet, but it is not good for one's public relations.

I once met a United States official whose job it had been to allocate United States surplus steel to other countries in one of those years after the Second World War when there was a world-wide steel famine. Allocating quotas is always an invidious job, and when, at last, this particular allocation had been completed and made public, my North American friend was sitting down to relax—so he thought. But, at that instant, a long-distance telephone call came through, with a furious voice at the far end of it. 'Canada speaking', said the voice. 'And pray why is not Canada in the United States steel quotas list?' 'Now I could not confess the truth to that angry Canadian', said my Estadosunidense friend in telling me the tale. 'The truth was that we had simply forgotten Canada. But how could I say that? He wouldn't have believed me, and, if I had convinced him, Canada would never have forgiven the United States. So I had to let the Canadian inquirer go on believing that we had left Canada out deliberately. The effect on Canadian–United States relations was, of course, pretty bad, but it was nothing like so bad as it would have been if I had let a Canadian know that Canada had been overlooked by Uncle Sam inadvertently.'

There it is. The giant's sheer size is always getting the

giant into trouble with people of normal stature. A Latin American politician has put the point in one short witty sentence. 'When the United States sneezes, Latin America gets influenza.'[1]

If disparity, in size were all that came between the United States and the Latin American republics, the problem of the relations between the different regions of the Western Hemisphere would not be the difficult problem that it is. The disparity could be overcome by a combination of tact on the North American side with a sense of humour on the Latin American side; and then harmony would be easily attainable. However, the disparity in size is not the whole trouble, as we well know. The malaise created by the disparity is dangerous because there are other causes of misunderstanding and of discord that are deeper and more serious. It is when these bigger issues come into play that a disparity in size, which, in itself, is, at best, no more than a joke and, at worst, no more than an irritant, generates friction that might shoot a spark into a powder-magazine.

The really grave issue is the question of the United States' attitude towards the movement for social justice. The Latin American workers and peasants are now demanding social justice 'with an insistence that makes this popular urge the leading force in Latin America'.[2] We have noted already that this movement is not confined to Latin America; it is world-wide. It is the first item on the present agenda of at least three-quarters of the human race. On this issue, where does the United States stand? Is she for social justice, or is she against it? I believe it would be no exaggeration to say that the United States' answer to this question, whatever her answer may be, is going to be decisive for her fate. If

[1] The Peruvian Aprista leader R. Prialé, quoted in *The United States and Latin America* (New York, 1959, The American Assembly of Columbia University), p. 182.

[2] H. L. Matthews, in *The United States and Latin America*, p. 169.

she were to declare against social justice, she would, in effect, be proclaiming herself to be one of the enemies of the human race, and we know what happens to these. Twice within a single lifetime, we have seen Germany defy the world and pay the just and inevitable penalty. If the United States were to dedicate herself irrevocably to the cause of wealth and vested interests, I believe History would sweep the United States out of the path of its onward march. 'If a free society cannot help the many who are poor, it cannot save the few who are rich', as President Kennedy put the truth epigrammatically in his Inaugural Address. If History were to brush away the Soviet Union too, in the same impartial sweep of her broom, there would be small consolation for the United States in that. So, on the issue of social justice, where does the United States stand today? This question is a world-wide one; but Latin America is the field in which the United States is going to be put to her acid test.

In Latin America, it is obvious, the United States' intentions are now suspect, and so are her motives even when she is taking action that, on the face of it, would be evidence that she had come down on the liberal side of the fence. 'Is this inference warrantable?' That is the question that the prospective Latin American beneficiaries ask themselves every time that the United States makes a motion to aid them 'Is the United States a sincere convert to the cause of social justice, or is this just another transparent manoeuvre in defence of the vested interests of the United States herself and the rest of the tiny affluent and satiated minority of mankind? Is the United States perhaps just doling out a minimum instalment of alimony to us as a less unpleasant alternative than "the wrath to come"? Is her true motive not the spontaneous generosity and idealism that she professes, but a haunting fear of those potent devils of flesh and blood who have taken over the role of the traditional devil of mythology? If this is the truth', say the Latin American critics of the United States, 'then United States aid is not the United States' own genuine gift. The parcel may have been made up in Washington, D.C., and the contents may have been paid for by the United States taxpayer, but the true donor is Premier Castro or Mr. Khrushchev or perhaps, in the last analysis, Karl Marx. If this timely devil had not been on the United States' tail, that parcel would never have been packed or have been delivered to us.' These are highly damaging insinuations; but they have not been made by Latin American critics only; they have been made by United States senators as well.

This happened *à propos*, for instance, of a statement, foreshadowing fresh aid from the United States to Latin America, that was made by President Eisenhower on 11 July 1960. In the press conference that immediately followed the delivery of this presidential message, the first question put to President Eisenhower was: Would the suggested co-operative action include Cuba under Premier Castro's régime? Mr. Eisenhower indicated that the answer was in the negative. Another question was whether United States aid to Latin America under the proposed new plan would be comparable to the Marshall Plan for Europe in character and in magnitude. President Eisenhower's answer was that it would not be 'anything remotely resembling' that, though some additions to current United States expenditure for the Latin American countries' benefit would probably be necessary. This pair of impromptu answers to key questions let the cat out of the bag. They implied that the motive for the proposed new United States *douceur* to all Latin American republics except Castro's Cuba was, not to aid them for the sake of helping them along their hard road, but to give them an inducement to refrain from following Castro's lead. It was surely also implied that the amount of the inducement was to be no more than the minimum estimated to be necessary for achieving this political purpose.

The New York Times, in its next morning's editorial, criticized the inadequacy of President Eisenhower's gesture mildly. It asked merely that, on the next occasion, the United States trumpet should give 'a more certain sound'. Democratic senators were less forbearing. On 8 August, Senator Mansfield called the President's perfunctory gesture 'a callous attempt to purchase favour in Latin America at a time when we are specially desirous of obtaining it'. On 11 August, Senator Fulbright characterized Secretary of State Herter's commendation of the new plan to the Senate Foreign Relations Committee as sounding 'a little like a death-bed confession'. On 4 September, Senator Humphrey observed that 'the light seems to dawn in the White House only when Cuba is already well down the Communist path'. After making full allowance for the play of party politics, one is still left with the impression that these damaging criticisms hit the mark. These opposition critics were, after all, patriotic United States citizens. And, if this was how President Eisenhower's gesture struck them, what must the impression have been in Latin America? In denying to Cuba, in advance, a share in the United States' projected gift, President Eisenhower had designated Premier Castro as being the true donor. Castro's Cuba saw and seized her opening. On 13 August 1960 *The Japan Times* carried a letter from the Cuban Ambassador in Tokyo submitting that 'the strategem is so clumsy that it will produce new friends for us and cause a great loss of international prestige for the powerful northern neighbour'.

If President Eisenhower was at fault, his fault lay, I should say, in reflecting too faithfully the current state of public opinion and feeling in the United States, instead of giving his havering countrymen a bold clear lead. A year later, the United States public's state of mind about Latin America was still ambiguous, if there is justice in the following characterization of it, in *The New York Times* of 11 June 1961, by a Harvard specialist in Latin American studies. Mr. John Plank. Discussing the difficulties that the Government and people of the United States would have to face in coping with the current crisis in Latin America and in United States–Latin American relations, Mr. Plank remarked that

'Perhaps most important among these difficulties is our deep-seated uneasiness in the presence of revolution, actual or immanent. For ourselves and for others we prize stability, continuity, institutionalized change; we are distrustful of abrupt shifts, violent, radical departure. Are we prepared, as a people, to adjust to the revolutionary tempest that is abroad today? If we are not, or if we cannot shortly prepare ourselves, we shall almost surely fail in our contest against totalitarianism.'

The United States public's response to the challenge of a swiftly developing crisis has been disconcertingly sluggish. The state of mind described by Mr. Plank seems no different from that reflected in Mr. Eisenhower's message a year back. In 1961 the people of the United States were still uncertain whether they wanted to play Mazzini's role or Metternich's role on the Western Hemisphere's twentieth-century political stage. There had, however, been one great and hopeful change, meanwhile, in the Administration at Washington. By the date at which Mr. Plank's article was published, President Kennedy had taken office, taken a line, and taken action. He had delivered his White House address of 13 March 1961 to Latin American diplomats, United States officials, and members of the United States Congress;

and he had delivered to the Congress in Washington his message of 14 March. In February 1962 I find that I still do not know where the people of the United States stand nowadays in their attitude towards the American Revolution. But we all know where the President stands. He has spoken out so boldly and plainly that he has left nobody any excuse for misunderstanding him.

Where do the people of the United States stand? Latin American observers naturally judge by the United States' recent record in Latin America. And undoubtedly there is evidence here to support the case made by Latin American sceptics against North American professions of virtue. I leave aside the allegation that the counter-revolution in Guatemala in 1954 was engineered by the United States Government at the instigation of the United Fruit Company. I have no information. Unfortunately there is no doubt about the United States Government's complicity in the abortive attempt at a counter-revolution in Cuba in 1961. This has been confessed by the Administration itself; and an attempt to subvert a foreign government with whom one is officially at peace is no less ugly when the deed is done, as it was in this case, by arming and unleashing a band of exiles than when it is done with one's own troops at their own risk, as it was in the Anglo–Franco–Israeli attack on Egypt in 1956. At the time of the Suez affair I was in Japan; at the time of the Cuba affair I was in the United States; and on this second occasion I was dismayed to find that, as far as I could make out, most people in the United States saw the Cuba fiasco as a failure in United States administrative efficiency and not as a moral issue, and that they were apparently insensitive to the effects of the incident on the moral standing of the United States, not only in the nineteen or twenty Latin American countries other than Cuba, but throughout the World.

World opinion is now a reality. It is also beginning to be a real force in world affairs; and, to its credit, world opinion detests and condemns nothing more vehemently than the use of force by a powerful country against a weaker one. Even people who disapprove of the character of the régime in the assaulted country will disapprove far more strongly of the international lawlessness and violence let loose in an attack on a weaker country by a stronger one in whatever circumstances. As long ago as the last years of the nineteenth century, my own country found herself in the dock on this count when she fought, conquered, and annexed the two Afrikaner Dutch republics. In Japan in 1956 the condemnation of the Anglo–Franco–Israeli attack on Egypt was instantaneous and universal. By analogy, I could estimate in 1961 what the World was feeling then about the Cuba affair, though the United States press served its country badly by virtually ignoring this aspect of it, which, in the long run, is going to be the most crucial aspect from the standpoint, not only of ethics, but also of United States national interests.

However, my own test of the attitude in the United States is neither Cuba nor Guatemala nor those invigorating embraces that some of the Latin American dictators have received, from time to time, from United States ambassadors accredited to them or from touring United States congressmen. Being a European, I find my test in the contrast, which I think I perceive, between the reaction of public feeling in the United States towards Communist Russia and its reaction towards Nazi Germany. In the United States today, public hostility towards the Soviet Union has risen to such a pitch that one finds people in the United States who would be willing to see their country fight an atomic war with the Soviet Union at the cost of condemning to death perhaps half the population of the United States, including the chauvinists' own children, not to speak of the slaughter of a proportionate number of innocent people in Russia and in the rest of the World as well. This temper in the United States in 1962 presents an amazing contrast to the temper in 1939, which was reflected in the passage of the neutrality legislation of that year. In 1939 the people of the United States were determined not to be involved in the war against the human race that Hitler was then on the point of launching.

How is this astonishing difference of reaction to be explained? Hitler was at least as wicked as the wickedest of the Communist leaders of Russia have been. Nazi Germany was at least as great a menace to the freedom of the human race as the Soviet Union may be. In my judgement, for what it is worth, the self-styled 'Free World' is in considerably less danger of falling under a totalitarian despotism in 1962 than it was in 1940. President Roosevelt saw the danger in 1940, and he was a consummate leader and educator of public opinion in his country. Yet it took the folly of Hitler and the Japanese militarists to drag the United States into participation in the Second World War on the anti-totalitarian side. Roosevelt, unassisted by the enemy, could not, I believe, have achieved this feat, superb statesman though he was. The weight of public indifference and inertia in the United States was still too great in 1941 for Roosevelt to have been able to make it budge if Hitler and the Japanese had left him to do the job single-handed.

Well, today, President Kennedy is having to rein in, with both hands, a war-horse that is fretting with eagerness to break into a charge, undeterred by the sight of the precipice immediately in front of its stamping hooves. How explain this total difference of temper in two situations that are surely comparable to each other? I believe I know the reason, and it is one that I find disquieting. I believe the reason why the people of the United States were unmoved by the aggressive march of Hitlerism was because they did not realize that this movement threatened their pockets. They do realize that Communism threatens their pockets. And, as I see it, this is why, when they spy Communism, they see red. I hope this diagnosis of mine is erroneous; for, if it were to prove to be correct, it would answer the fateful question 'Where does the United States stand on the momentous present-day issue between vested interests and social justice?' The answer would be a lamentable one. It would be that the paramount aim of the people of the United States is the protection of their own vested interests, and that they are not concerned for social justice except in so far as this can be made to serve a purpose that is, in truth, the opposite of what social justice stands for.

As I have said, I do not think the people of the United States have yet committed themselves to this stand irrevocably. Their decision is, I believe, still hovering on the razor's edge. This is why the stand taken by President Kennedy at this juncture is so important and so encouraging. The question of what is being done is not the only one that matters when the business on the agenda is aid to Latin America from the United States. Even the question of how much is being done does not cover the whole issue. The answers to the questions why it is being done and how it is going to be done are not less important. The answer to the question why is the test of the United States' sincerity. The answer to the question how will be the test of Latin America's liberalism.

The ultimate answer to the question why has been given by President Kennedy. The United States must give aid to Latin America because to do this is a good thing in itself. Why is it a good thing? Because it promotes the cause of social justice. And why should this cause be promoted? Well, justice, and the well-being that it brings with it in so far as it is achieved in the social field, are two of the absolute values in human life. So the cause of social justice is certainly a good cause; but, if one is a citizen of the United States, one has also a special reason for promoting it. This special reason is a national and an historical one. The ideal of social justice is the ideal of the American Revolution.

In launching 'the Alliance for Progress' between the United States and the Latin American republics, President Kennedy has nailed the colours of the American Revolution to his mast-head. In his White House Address of 13 March 1961 the President made his stand clear.

'The revolutions which gave us birth', he reminded his mixed North American and Latin American audience, 'ignited, in the words of Thomas Paine, "a spark never to be extinguished". And across vast turbulent continents these American ideals still stir Man's struggle for national independence and individual freedom. But, as we welcome the spread of the American Revolution to other lands, we must also remember that our own struggle—the revolution which began in Philadelphia in 1776 and in Carácas in 1811—is not yet finished. Our hemisphere's mission is not yet complete. . . . Let us once again awaken our American Revolution until it guides the struggles of people everywhere.'

Here President Kennedy is surely speaking the American Revolution's authentic language. Confirmatory texts could be found on every other page of Jefferson's works; and Jefferson's theme has been summed up by Emerson in six famous syllables: 'the shot heard round the World'. Perhaps the most impressive witness to the continuing momentum of the American Revolution is Metternich. He bore witness to the American Revolution's principles in denouncing them to the Czar Alexander *à propos* of the promulgation of the Monroe Doctrine.

'These United States of America', Metternich lamented, 'have astonished Europe by a new act of revolt, more unprovoked, fully as audacious, and no less dangerous than the former. . . . In . . . fostering revolutions wherever they show themselves, in regretting those which have failed, in extending a helping hand to those which seem to prosper, they lend new strength to the apostles of sedition, and reanimate the courage of every conspirator. If this flood of pernicious example should extend over the whole of America, what would become of our religious and political institutions, of the moral force of our governments, and of the conservative system which has saved Europe from complete dissolution?'[1]

But, Mr. Toynbee, I am afraid you have gone senile and muddled up your names and dates. The voice that you have just been quoting can only be the voice of John Foster Dulles bewailing to President Eisenhower Mr. Khrushchev's championship of the Cuban revolution. Well, Mr. Chairman, you might think so, but I have verified my reference. This really is the voice of a nineteenth-century Austrian statesman, denouncing that subversive instrument the Monroe Doctrine to an earlier autocrat of all the Russias than the present incumbent.

Revolution is a mettlesome horse. One must either ride it or else be trampled to death by it. The Hapsburg Monarchy and the Czardom have both been trampled to death within the last half-century. But how did a revolutionary-minded Russian acrobat manage subsequently to vault into the saddle? He found the saddle vacant; so, by the date at which the present Russian rider lodged himself there, the original American rider must have dismounted. Can the United States recapture her revolutionary birth-

[1] Metternich, quoted by Dexter Perkins in *The United States and Latin America* (Baton Rouge, 1961, Louisiana State University Press), pp. 46–47.

right? President Kennedy has proclaimed this as his ambition for her. Is the United States going to take the leap, or
is she going to stall? Her destiny hangs on her choice; for
to linger dismounted in the arena is to court death—especially in our day, when the world arena is rapidly contracting,
so that the trampling horse is thundering round it in ever
narrowing circles.

President Kennedy's approach to the United States' problem calls for an abandonment of John Foster Dulles's attitude to revolution and a resumption of Jefferson's attitude.
This point has been well taken by authoritative commenta-
tors in the United States. John Plank, in the article in *The
New York Times* of 11 June 1961 from which I have already
quoted, points out that 'an invocation of the Monroe Doctrine, a brandishing of our arms, will do little to stop the
flood of ideas and ideologies that is now, as never before,
pouring in upon Latin America'. Like microbes, ideas ignore
man-made frontiers; and, as a shield for vested interests, the
Monroe Doctrine is about as ineffective as the Holy
Alliance was as a shield against revolution at the time when
the Monroe Doctrine was promulgated. If the present
'Alliance for Progress' were ever to degenerate into a Holy
Alliance, it would assuredly suffer the Holy Alliance's
ignominious fate.

'We must identify ourselves', Mr. Plank says to his North
American compatriots, 'with the revolutionary currents that
are abroad in our hemisphere today.' He advises his compatriots to regard the forces of change now at work in the
Hemisphere 'as opportunities to be exploited rather than as
evils to be checked'. He tells them that they must be willing
to support, and even to encourage, much more governmental
intervention in the economies of Latin American countries
than most North Americans would be prepared to tolerate
at home. And they must not let themselves be put off by

the bogy-word 'socialism'. The same line of thought is followed out by another North American student of Latin America, Mr. Herbert Matthews.[1] This North American observer points out that, in Latin America, 'free enterprise' has been discredited by the unedifying way in which it has been practised there by business men, native and foreign, including some North American business interests. He underlines 'the hopelessness of applying economic orthodoxy to Latin America'. He justly commends Mr. Nixon for having learned, on his stormy passage through Latin America in 1958, that the strength of the current revolutionary movement for social justice there has not been appreciated either by public opinion in the United States or by the privileged minority in the Latin American countries themselves. Mr. Matthews gives warning that a 'stability that keeps military dictators or oligarchies in power is a lid clamped down on an explosive brew'.

'Latin Americans were not, and are not, looking to us', Mr. Matthews tells his compatriots, 'to lead a crusade against Communism, but to help them meet their real and pressing social, economic, and political problems. . . . The danger seems far away, and, since they know we are defending ourselves and our own way of life first and foremost, they are not impressed. . . . The millions who accepted poverty and misery as unavoidable no longer do so.'

And the price paid by the masses for what has been done for them by Communism in Russia and China does not appal 'a Colombian or Brazilian or Guatemalan peasant who asks how he and his family could be any worse off than they are today'.

[1] In *The United States and Latin America* (New York, December 1959, The American Assembly of Columbia University), pp. 143–193.

As Mr. Stevenson has put it,[1] 'the underprivileged have been caught up in the winds of change. They are tired of promises; they want action, results—not for their grand-children but for themselves.'

In the light of these shrewd and expert counsels, it is noteworthy that President Kennedy, in his White House address of 13 March 1961, characterized his 'Alliance for Progress' as being 'the first large-scale inter-American effort to attack the social barriers which block economic progress'; and that he followed this up, next day, in his message to the Congress in Washington, by declaring explicitly: 'The fund which I am requesting today will be devoted to social progress.' In the same message, the President made the crucial point that 'economic growth without social progress lets the great majority of the people remain in poverty, while a privileged few reap the benefits of rising abundance'.

Thus the United States' aid to Latin America under the Kennedy Plan is directed to a clearly defined objective; and, for the United States, this raises a delicate political question. If a United States plan for Latin America embodies a policy, does not this amount to an interference in the domestic affairs of the Latin American countries? And is not this a breach of the United States' pledge to abstain from inter-fering?

The Kennedy Plan does constitute interference. This cannot be denied; but it is something that the United States is unable to avoid. She is unable because the reason why her aid amounts to interference lies, not in her action itself, but in the situation in the Latin American field of it. If all parties in each of the Latin American countries were at one in desiring social justice, no political problem would arise. But it is only a majority there that desires social justice and demands it, and the minority is not only obstinately recal-

[1] In an article in *The New York Times* of 6 August 1961.

citrant; it is also still politically powerful, in spite of the
inroads that have been made on its traditional dominance
within the lifetime of the present generation. In the domestic
politics of many Latin American countries, as in those of
many other countries, different classes, parties, and movements are at sixes and sevens; and, in such a situation,
foreign aid is bound to be discriminating. It will give one
side an advantage, and the opposing side a disadvantage, in
the domestic political struggle. Even the wagging of an
intruding puppy dog's tail would have this interventionary
effect; the swingeing of a great dane's flail will be proportionately potent.

The only way in which the United States could make
sure of being one hundred per cent. true to her pledge not
to intervene in the Latin American countries' domestic
affairs would be for her to withdraw into isolation and to
leave Latin America to try to work out her own salvation
unaided. But this would be to solve the problem of United
States–Latin American relations by reducing it *ad absurdum*.
Any such solution would be equally inimical to the interests,
and contrary to the desires, of the United States and her
Latin American associates alike. It would be tantamount to
abandoning the field to Communism—which, as Mr. Stevenson has truly said,[1] is 'a magnet that attracts and will continue to draw unhappy people as long as the spokesmen of
other political philosophies seem capable only of talk, and
can point to no action to right wrongs'. A solution that is
to serve the common interests of the Western Hemisphere
cannot be found in any philosophy of inaction. The right
solution is surely for both parties to the Hemisphere partnership to recognize that North American intervention in Latin
American affairs is an unavoidable consequence of North
American aid, and to deal with this fact of life by assigning

[1] In *The New York Times*, 6 August 1961.

to each of the Latin American nations the responsibility for determining, in its own case, what the effect of North American intervention is to be.

This is the solution that President Kennedy propounded from the start. 'Our greatest challenge comes from within', he declared in his White House address. 'Only the determined efforts of the American nations themselves can bring success to this effort', he said. 'Each Latin nation must formulate long-range plans for its own development. . . . These plans will be . . . the basis for the allocation of outside resources.' And he enlarged on this point next day in his message to the Congress in Washington.

'Priorities', he said, 'will depend not merely on need but on the demonstrated readiness of each government to make the institutional improvements which promise lasting social progress. . . . Funds will not be allocated until the operating agency receives assurances that the country being aided will take those measures necessary to ensure that the particular project brings the social progress.'

These provisos place the responsibility for deciding to make, or not to make, use of the new fund for progress on those shoulders on which this responsibility ought to rest. The fund is earmarked for the promotion of social justice; but no Latin American country is going to be constrained to promote social justice by drawing on the fund, because the choice between participating and not participating rests with each of the Latin American governments. Suppose that some Latin American country has the misfortune to find itself under a government that declines to participate because this government's objective is to obstruct social justice, not to promote it. Well, that would be just too bad from the standpoint of the great majority of the people of that country, who would, no doubt, be as eager for social justice as any of their neighbours. It would be too bad; yet this frustration would be not altogether undeserved, and it would certainly not be irremediable. It would be not undeserved because the saying that 'every country gets the government that it deserves' has some truth in it. The situation would also not be irremediable, because a nation does have the power to change a government, even a dictatorial government, whose rule it has been tolerating. Every government, bad or good, weak or strong, is always on sufferance only. It is open to a bad government in a Latin American country to continue to set its face against social justice at the risk of being hurled from power by its own indignant subjects. And, of course, there is an open road for any régime that stands for social justice to promote its worthy aim by taking advantage of 'the Alliance for Progress'.

The assumption underlying the Kennedy Plan is that social justice is the objective of the great majority of the people of Latin America; that this majority is going to make its will prevail; and that the movement for social justice is therefore 'the wave of the future'. But social justice cannot be promoted in Latin America without some drastic changes in the distribution of wealth, and therefore also of political power; and these changes will not be achieved without a struggle, because they will be changes at the expense of the vested interests of a privileged and powerful minority.

In some Latin American countries the present taxation of wealth is inequitably light when measured by present North American, not to speak of British, standards. How can the North American taxpayer be asked by his own government to contribute to a fund for the betterment of conditions in Latin America when Latin American taxpayers, richer than he is, are being let off by their own internal revenue far more lightly? And how could the authority that is to administer the fund recommend a grant in aid of agriculture for a country in which land-reform is still inadequate, if not altogether lacking? In such a situation the effect of the grant would be to increase the wealth of a handful of already inordinately wealthy *latifundarios*, and this would be, not to mitigate social injustice, but to accentuate it, as Mr. Kennedy observed in his message of 14 March 1961 to the Congress in Washington. How, again, can any grant be administered honestly and efficiently by a country's civil service if this public administrative staff is full of sinecure-holders and political place-men? The grant in aid will run into the sands if the professional standards of the local civil service are too low for doing the job; and, in such a situation, a *sine qua non* of aid will be civil service reform.

Above all, 'the Alliance for Progress' requires political leaders who are statesmen, not 'politicians' in the uncomplimentary usage of the word. Mr. Stevenson, who knows Latin America well, and who made his latest tour there only last year, has expressed a hopeful view in an article in *The New York Times* of 6 August 1961. 'The leaders of the Americas know today', he said, 'that they must identify themselves with essential changes that are demonstrably for the benefit of all the people.' One might add a list of other necessary qualifications for leadership. Leaders must be honest, they must be public-spirited, they must have vision, they must have enthusiasm, and each and all of these obligatory virtues must be fortified by common sense and by sound judgement. In their enthusiasm for social justice, the statesmen who are going to put 'the Alliance for Progress' into operation must not lose sight of the continuing need to keep economic progress going, since, if this flags, the movement for social justice will be debilitated by being starved of the requisite economic sustenance. The crucial problem for statesmanship in Latin America is the practical one of promoting the movement for social justice and the movement for economic development simultaneously without allowing either movement to get out of step with the other. In the first of these lectures I called attention to this point by citing some recent instances in which one or the other of these two movements has been promoted to the complementary movement's detriment. The cases that I cited suggest that a loss of balance, in whichever direction, is apt to bring disaster with it. This Latin American experience is one that ought to be taken to heart by all the authorities that will be sharing the responsibility for administering the new fund.

The initiative has come from the United States; the follow-up must come from Latin America. The key-word here is 'self-help'. Self-help is not only brought within the reach of every participating Latin American country by the self-determination for which the Kennedy Plan provides; self-help is also one of the moral obligations that the boon of self-determination creates for nations that accept it.

What are the prospects? What light is thrown on them by the proceedings at the conference held on 5–17 August 1961 at Punta del Este in Uruguay? The United States Government's point of view was expressed once again, and, as before, with great clarity, in President Kennedy's message to the conference and in the opening speech of Mr. Douglas Dillon, the head of the United States delegation, who took up the President's points and developed them. The President reaffirmed the need for continuing revolutionary action in the Western Hemisphere 'for the freedom and self-fulfil-ment of Man', and he indicated, once again, that this would call for changes in traditional policies, and for the subordination of vested interests to the general public interest, in the United States as well as in the Latin American countries. He once again raised the questions of expanded export markets and greater market stability for the major primary

products—questions which had not received a sympathetic
hearing in the United States in the past. In the same sentence, he also raised the question of economic integration
within Latin America—a question which, in the past, had
been a stumbling-block for Latin American governments.
President Kennedy also called, once again, for

'full recognition of the right of all the people to share fully
in our progress. For', he said again, 'there is no place in
democratic life for institutions which benefit the few while
denying the needs of the many, even though the elimination
of such institutions may require far-reaching and difficult
changes such as land-reform and tax-reform and a vastly
increased emphasis on education and health and housing.
Without these changes', President Kennedy declared, 'our
common effort cannot succeed.'

There was never any doubt of the United States Administration's firm intention to give massive financial support to
any plans for effectively pursuing these purposes that the
Latin American governments might put forward. And, while
the conference was in session, the United States delegation's
hand was strengthened by the news that the Senate in Washington had rejected an amendment to the President's foreign
aid bill that would have struck out of it the power to borrow
on long term for raising funds for carrying out the bill's
purposes. In the 'Declaration to the Peoples of America'
that was signed on 17 August 1961 by all delegations to the
conference except the Cuban, the United States Government's pledge of financial aid was embodied explicitly. But
the conference dispersed without any correspondingly ex-
plicit pledge on the part of the other signatories to the
declaration that they were equally in earnest. The statement
of aims in the declaration contained all that could have

been desired by the most ardent champion of social justice. The question that still, I think, remains open concerns the means of implementation on the Latin American governments' side.

In this connexion, Mr. Dillon, in his opening address, had underlined the importance of establishing an Inter-American Committee on Development Plans as 'an instrument of great value in facilitating the systematic and sustained provision of outside assistance for soundly conceived progress'. The experience of the implementation of the Marshall Plan for Europe tells powerfully in favour of setting up a strong steering committee of this kind. At least, this seems to have been one of the principal causes of the Marshall Plan's success. It was therefore natural and proper that the structure and powers of the proposed committee should have been the main focus of discussion at the Punta del Este conference. It is perhaps also ominous that this was the point on which the United States delegation met with opposition. The smaller Latin American countries were in agreement with the United States in wishing to establish such a committee and to make it a strong one; the larger Latin American countries wished to water this proposal down; and the terms of the declaration of 17 August 1961 seem to indicate that, in this conflict of wills, the larger Latin American countries' wishes prevailed. In this document the word 'committee' does not appear. All that is said is that 'independent and highly qualified experts will be made available to Latin American countries in order to assist in formulating and examining national development plans'.

If I had been the head of the Cuban delegation, Major Guevara, I suppose I should have been pleased at this victory of the larger Latin American countries' nationalism. I should have been pleased because I should have reckoned that 'the Alliance for Progress' was having its teeth drawn before these had had time to sprout. I should have calculated that this would diminish the chances of success for this new project for achieving social justice in Latin America by peaceful agreement. And then I should have licked my lips. For, if social justice is not going to be attained by the American democratic revolutionary method, then the Russian Communist revolutionary method is likely to have its chance, not just in Cuba, but in other Latin American countries too. This is likely, because the demand for social justice is one that will not be denied.

Of course, the implementation of 'the Alliance for Progress' has only just begun. We cannot yet forecast its prospects. I do not want to end on a pessimistic note, but I am bound to end on a note of interrogation.

WORKS CONSULTED

American Assembly of Columbia University: symposium: *The United States and Latin America* (New York, 1959).

Benham, F., and Holley, H. A.: *A Short Introduction to the Economy of Latin America* (London, 1960, Oxford University Press, for the Royal Institute of International Affairs).

Benitez, Jaime: *The United States, Cuba, and Latin America* (script of address delivered 6–7 March 1961).

Benitez, Jaime: *The United States, Cuba, and Latin America* (Santa Barbara, Cal., 1961, Fund for the Republic) [written after the abortive landings in Cuba in April 1961].

Bryson, Lyman, introducer of symposium: *Social Change in Latin America Today* (New York, 1961, Harpers, for the Council on Foreign Relations).

Committee for Economic Development: *Cooperation for Progress in Latin America* (New York, April 1961).

Drucker, P. F.: 'A Plan for Revolution in Latin America', in *Harper's Magazine*, July 1961, pp. 31–38.

Ellis, M. S., and Wallich, H. C., editors of symposium: *Economic Development for Latin America* (London, 1961, Macmillan).

Hirschman, A. O., editor of symposium: *Latin American Issues* (New York, 1961, Twentieth Century Fund).

Johnson, J. J.: *Political Change in Latin America: The Emergence of the Middle Sectors* (Stanford, Cal., 1958, Stanford University Press).

Kennedy, President: *Address at a Reception for Latin American Diplomats, Officials, and Members of Congress,* held at the White House, 13 March 1961 (1961, U.S. Information Service).

Kennedy, President: *Message to the U.S. Congress on Latin America,* 14 March 1961.

Perkins, Dexter: *The United States and Latin America* (Baton Rouge, 1961, Louisiana State University Press).

Plank, J.: 'What Policy for Latin America?' (*The New York Times,* 11 June 1961).

Stevenson, Adlai: Excerpts from report of tour, in 1961, of ten South American countries (*The New York Times,* 6 August 1961).